My Life's Adventures From A to Z

Frederick E. Sowders

authorHOUSE®

AuthorHouse™
1663 Liberty Drive
Bloomington, IN 47403
www.authorhouse.com
Phone: 1-800-839-8640

Published by AuthorHouse 9/4/2013

ISBN: 978-1-4918-1547-2 (sc)

THIS BOOK IS DEDICATED
TO
MY HIGH SCHOOL
SWEETHEART
AND
LIFE LONG COMPANION

RETHA M. ROBERTSON
SOWDERS

I WANT TO THANK MY WONDERFUL
WIFE OF 55 YEARS

ALL THAT SHE HAS HAD TO
TOLERATE

AS SHE RAISED A FAMILY AND
HUSBAND AT THE SAME TIME

I THANK HER MORE THAN SHE WILL
EVER KNOW
FOR ALL SHE HAS TAUGHT ME
OVER THE YEARS

Illustrations by
Ruby Fletcher Robertson

A WONDERFUL FRIEND
ALWAYS ENCOURAGING
ME WITH MY STORIES

WELCOME TO THE FAMILY

Ruby married my wife's brother
Daniel Robertson
June 9, 2006

Editing By
Retha M. Sowders

And

Debbie Sowders

ACKNOWLEDGEMENT
TO THOSE THAT HAVE HELPED
ME ALONG LIFE'S PATHWAY

STEVEN SOWDERS
JOY R. SOWDERS LINEHAN
LINDA SUSAN SOWDERS HALL

MY WONDERFUL CHILDREN

THANKS TO EACH OF YOU
FOR YOUR ENCOURAGEMENT
IN WRITING MY LIFE STORIES

THIS WORK HAS TAKEN A LONG
TIME TO COME TO FRUITATION.
IT IS MY DESIRE TO PASS ON WHAT
I'VE EXPERIENCED, THAT THOSE IN FUTURE
GENERATIONS CAN SHARE IT WITH ME.

LIFE IS A SUTTLE THING, STRONG
YET FRAIL.
AS A CHILD THERE IS NO THOUGHT
OF WHAT MAY LIE AHEAD
THERE IS ONLY THE NEED OF THE MOMENT

IF I COULD PASS ON A SIMPLE PHRASE
"HOLD ON TO WHAT IS NOW,
MAKE IT LAST A LIFE TIME
DO ALL THAT IS AFFORDABLE
WITH EACH PASSING DAY".

'TIL, AT LAST YOU REACH THE POINT IN TIME THAT
YOU CAN DO NO MORE, REMEMBER EVERY
EVENT AND SAVOR EACH MOMENT
OF AN EXCITING PAST

I DO THAT EACH DAY AS I WRITE
RELIVING MOMENTS FROM MY MIND
THERE IS ALWAYS MORE THAT I WANT
TO TELL TO EACH OF YOU.

TABLE OF CONTENTS

Section I
Childhood

Section II
Life

Section III
Flying

Section IV
Special People

Section V
Racing

SECTION I

CHILDHOOD

BUILDING FENCE

There was talk of purchasing a milk cow after we moved to the ten-acre farm and after building Grandma Cora's house nearby. A fence needed to be built too along the gravel road to keep the cow in the field, since the old fence had been removed.

I remember Dad and his brother Ethel, talking about the need of a fence around Grandma's plot. Stakes were set out for each fence post that would be needed. I was too little to help with the digging but with each passing day, I saw new holes appear for the designated fence.

Soon fence posts appeared and the task of setting the posts was near. Since I was too small to handle a shovel or do the tamping of the dirt as it was placed back in the hole, my job was to hold the post up straight, while dirt was placed in the hole around it. I do remember holding a level against the posts. I am sure my Dad could tell that I wanted a hand in this project.

When all of the posts had been set it was now time to place the barbed wire on the posts. At the beginning of a run the wire was wrapped around the post and nailed firmly in place. The spool of wire was attached to the back of the 1929 Model A truck, so as to let the spool spin slowly as the truck moved up the fence row.

Upon reaching the corner, the spool was laid on the ground and a chain was attached to the back end of the truck and hooked to the strand of barbed wire. The truck was moved ever so slowly to put tension on the wire.

When tight the wire was nailed to every post. When this was done the procedure was repeated for the other two strands of wire.

This was enough to keep the cow from wondering about. Soon as one section was completed, the same was done on the next straight section.

No gates were installed. Instead, if one wished to cross the fence the person had to duck down and move across between the two strands of barbed wire. Many times, when in hurry, or not paying attention the barbs would catch into ones clothing. Some times it would dig into the flesh. I still have faint scars from not being careful when moving though the fence.

When getting water from the outside well for Grandmother Cora, from our house, we children had to cross the fence going and coming back.

As I write these stories, it seems I was at Grandma Cora's house a lot. I did spend a lot of time there as Mother and Dad both worked when I was young. It was a natural thing to go where I could talk or play near an adult.

I spent many hours playing on the dirt bank in front of the house, which bordered the gravel road. I didn't have toys bought from a store, but had tread spools or a block of wood fashioned into a crude truck.

Still, I was happy and spent many wonderful hours on that bank.

Then I always had stick horses to collect and fashion into many designs from the nearby sassafras trees along the graveled road.

Some times, I would spend hours collecting wild cherries. Hour after hour my playmates and I spent our time climbing trees to eat until ones heart was content. You could never eat enough of the cherries to become sick. I know because I ate hundreds of thousands and never got sick.

I enjoyed growing up in the country. I loved to be out side doing things. I enjoyed having a vivid imagination while being so close to nature.

CRACKLIN CORNBREAD

I am five years old and this is the first autumn that we are on our new farm. A lot of different things are happening. Dad had built a pond. He had fenced it in and had two hogs in the enclosure to help seal the pond bottom. The hogs grew like weeds. They were fun to watch as we walk up to the pen. Many times they would be out in the middle of the water hole and when they heard us, they come rushing out of the water and mud to the trough where Dad put their food.

They always seem to be hungry. They almost fight to get a spot closest to the point where Dad will pour feed into the trough. Little did they know, or I know, that they were going to be our winter supply of meat.

Months pass and the hogs grow larger. Finally it was late October and one Saturday morning I get out of bed and after having breakfast, I asked Mother, where is Dad. She told me that Dad was going to butcher the hogs today.

It is still early in the morning and I can see my breath each time I breathe out. I was a huffing and a puffing by the time I get to the hog pen. There is a fifty five-gallon barrel of water sitting on stones and there is a good fire going under it. The water is so hot that it is steaming. Looking further beyond the barrel I can see the two hogs. They have already been killed.

Dad and Uncle Ethel are putting a stick, almost like a single tree, between the back two legs of one of the hogs. For those that do not know what a single tree is, it is used to hitch a horse to a plow or some other type of farm equipment. It is about three feet long and larger in diameter in the middle than it is on both ends. On each end is a metal band around the wood and fixed to this, is a steel ring about two inches in diameter. In the center there is a band of metal around the wood and it also has a steel ring attached to it.

The horse's harness is hooked to each end of the single tree and the farm implement is hooked to the center ring. This is used for many jobs on a farm, such as plowing fields, pulling sleds or what ever is needed.

What Dad was using was about the same length but it was sharpened on each end. In the center of the crosspiece was a place to hook a chain. The ends of the crosspiece were inserted inside of the tendon of the hog's hind legs.

Dad has an A frame standing over the barrels and there is a block and tackle hooked to it right over the barrel of hot water. The block is hooked to the stick between the hog's back two feet and they are pulling on the rope to raise the pig over the barrel.

Wow, they get the pig up in the air over the barrel. I have never seen anything like this before. What the heck, is going to happen next? Slowly the hog is lowered into the barrel of hot water. Dad grabs a shovel and starts scooping ashes out from the edges of the fire. Next, he throws them into the water. He does this, two or three times. Hey, what is going to happen next? I am sure my eyes are just about to bug out of my head. I didn't know that ashes contain lye, which helps to loosen the hair on the hog.

The hog is raised up about three feet and Dad grabs a hand full of the hog's hair and it comes right off. Seeing this, the hog is raised even higher and then lowered outside the barrel. The rope is disconnected and everyone jumps in and the hog is dragged several feet away, where the workers begin using a large bladed knife and start scrapping the hair off the hog. I grab a knife and get right in there with the best of them, doing what I see being done.

Soon most of the hair is removed. Sometimes there are areas that did not get enough heat to loosen the hair. When this happens, a bran sack is dipped into the barrel of hot water. Then it is quickly placed on the area where the hair is still firm. Boy did it steam while you were waiting

7

on the heat to take effect. Soon the sack was removed and the scraping begins again. Soon the first hog is scarped clean.

The process begins again on the second hog. Only this time it seems to go quicker. The water is hotter and there are not as many places that have to have extra heat applied. There are areas on both hogs that still have some hair here and there, particularly, around the feet and the ears. These are hard places to get all of the hair removed. Sometimes the hair is shaved off. The knives are very sharp and the hair is just cut off close to the skin. You could tell these areas as you rub your hand across the skin.

I thought I had seen it all with the scalding and removing the hair. I ain't seen anything yet. After the last hog is scraped the barrel of hot water is tipped over allowing the water to run out across the ground. The fire is put out and now the first hog is once again connected to the block and tackle. It is hoisted up in the air and swings gently back and forth.

Dad selects the knife that he likes best and begins to rub it slowly, back and forth on a whetstone. He gives the blade eight or ten strokes on each side of the blade. Testing it on his thumb he is satisfied and goes to the hog and turns it until the belly is toward him.

Starting at the highest point between the hog's legs he begins to cut through the flesh. After making the first incision he inserts two fingers of his left hand into the cut and uses them to support the meat as he continues to cut the belly open.

The knife is drawn along the rib cage; Dad turns and picks up a hacksaw. He cuts through the bone down to the neck area. Laying the hacksaw aside he uses his knife to finish the midline cut. The head is removed and placed in a large pan that Mother uses for washing dishes. It is set aside and Dad begins to remove all of the insides that will not be saved for eating.

The hog is now in two pieces. These are taken down and it is time for the second hog to be cleaned. When the second carcass is gutted and cut into two pieces, we are ready to do what??—I have not the foggiest idea. I have never seen this done before.

Dad made up a rough table by laying several planks on two sawhorses. Dad and Uncle Ethel pick up one of the hog halves and lay it on the table. Dad finds his favorite knife and out comes the whetstone again. He hones the edge until he is again satisfied with the sharpness of the blade.

Dad started with the rear of the hog and deftly begins to cut the ham off. He takes his time but he seems to know exactly what he is doing. With sure cuts he continued, raising the ham with his left hand as he worked. One final cut and he lifted the ham and laid it to one side. He did the same thing with the shoulder cut and placed it by the ham.

Dad tells me the belly is where bacon comes from. He positions his knife and cuts the fatty part of the belly off and lays it with the other cuts. With a slight smile Dad tells me that we will enjoy bacon all winter. This he lays with the other cut pieces.

The truck is backed up close to the cutting table and the meat is transferred to the bed of the truck. As Dad cuts up the remaining hog halves each cut is placed onto the truck bed as well.

When everything has been cleaned up it is time to head for the house. I am tired and I am sure the days' work is done. WRONG!!!!!!! When we got to the house Dad backed the truck up to the smokehouse and once again set up his sawhorse table. All of the cuts of meat were placed inside, on the table. Dad was very specific that the cuts of meat were not to touch each other. He explained to me that the meat would be left in the smoke shed over night. The meat would be allowed to cool over night before any thing else is done.

Now our day is over and all that is left to do is to do the daily chores. The cow has to be fed and milked, and the chickens fed. When this is completed we turned to the house and mother has supper ready. Boy, am I tired, for a five-year-old, as this had been a long day. Little did I know that though I was tired and ready for an early bedtime Dad and Mother still has many things to do, before they could retire.

Muslin cloth came from somewhere and was placed on the table. Black pepper, red pepper and salt mix is set on the table as well. Sugar, (both white and brown), were the final ingredients in the mixture that will be rubbed all over the meat and in every opening. Straight pins and a light cord or string is found and put on the table as well. Mother and Dad begin to pour each of the ingredients into a large dishpan. I don't know what the measures of each are but there is a lot less of the red pepper added.

When all of this has been mixed it is covered and set aside. Their day finished Mother and Dad head for their bedroom. I eagerly jumped into my bed and was asleep in an instant. I know now, that another full day lay ahead for us; I just did not know how full it is going to be.

When I woke the next morning, Dad and Mother had already done the morning chores and are getting ready to sugar cure the meat. The white muslin cloth is measured out large enough to wrap the piece of meat several times. Next, newspaper or white wrapping paper is laid on the muslin cloth. The paper must completely encase the cut of meat. This is then covered with a liberal sprinkling of the salt mixture. Then the cut of meat is laid on this with the skin side down onto the salt mixture. A liberal amount of the salt mixture is then rubbed into every nook and cranny of the meat.

But before the wrapping and sugar cure mixture is placed on the meat, each and every piece, is trimmed of excess fat. This is placed into a large pan and soon it is filled to the top. Fat of all shapes and sizes is being piled on the pan.

Soon it is overrunning and another pan is produced and soon the second pan is full as well. There is fat everywhere. Still Dad cut it off. For what I did not know at the time. I must add there was another pan that contained meat with some fat. This I later learned was to be ground into sausage. I was told that there should be about a fifty-fifty mixture of meat and fat.

Dad soon had all of the different cuts of meat trimmed and ready to wrap.

Paper is carefully folded around the meat, followed by the muslin cloth. Pins are used to hold the cloth tightly in place. A strong string cradle is tied about the bundle so the cut of meat could be hung up in the same position, as it was when it was on the animal. If the meat is hung upside down or crossways the fluids remaining in the meat will cause it to spoil.

After the hams, shoulders, bacon slabs are ready to be hung, its time to smoke them. If the meat is not smoked it is hung in a cool place until needed.

We began carrying all of the wrapped meat to the smokehouse. Dad hangs each one on a nail that had been driven into the rafters. After several trips all of the wrapped bundles are inside the smoke shed.

There is no floor in the shed, just dirt. Just inside the door Dad begins to build a fire. When it is burning nicely Dad told me to carry several pieces of green hickory sticks and put them just outside the door. The hickory wood has been cut into fourteen to sixteen inch lengths. There are all sizes, from one-quarter inch branches to sticks about three inches in diameter.

Dad picks up his hatchet and cuts slivers off the larger pieces. These and the smaller branches he puts on the fire. Smoke begins to roll. The wood is still green and does not want to burn, very well. Dad has a hot fire to begin with, to get the hickory to burn.

Now back to the house and my job was to cut the fat into about one inch cubes. I cut and I cut, then I cut some more. It seemed like forever that I cut that fat. Finally Mother and Dad joined me and still it took a long time to get it all cut up into cubes.

The next day when I got up Dad already had our big black kittle setting on stones behind the smoke house and a fire started underneath it. Dad had already placed one wash pan full of the cubed fat into the kittle. As the kittle got hotter the fat began to liquefy. In other words the grease was slowly being released from the cubes of fat.

Slowly, I mean really slowly the liquid fat which is really lard, is extracted. Slowly, ever so slowly what was a white cube is turned into a crackling.

When the cracklings turned brown Dad would take a sieve and slowly shim them from the liquid lard and place them in another dish pan. This continued until there were no cracklings left in the kittle.

Dad then began dipping the liquid lard into a five gallon bucket that had a lid to fit it. The bucket was soon filled. The process started all over again.

I remember we had three large buckets of lard for Mother to use in her cooking.

Now the cracklings had to be taken care of. Mother started filling quart jars with cracklings. As soon as mother got one jar full Dad would take a small ladle and pour liquid lard into the jar. This continued until every crackling was safely put away in a jar. The jars were left outside overnight to allow the lard to cool and harden.

During the winter I know we had cornbread with cracklings in the cornbread. It was really good and it was always a treat to have crackling cornbread.

I would like to have some of mother's cornbread with those wonderful cracklings. I can still taste them when I recall those moments.

We may have been poor but we sure ate well at the same time.

Dad's Whistle

The first summer after moving to the ten acre farm, I stayed very close to the house and barn. Soon I developed a more secure feeling and would wonder farther and farther up over the hill in the back and even go as far as the old barn that was on the property.

At times I was out of ear shot of the house. That is, I was far enough away that I could not hear mother or dad call for me.

Soon dad devised a whistle with his lips that I could hear at the farthest point of the farm. It was a high pitch tone that I knew immediately that I was to come to the house.

It never failed. If I was wanted at the house dad would give his whistle and I would come running. All of my life on the farm I responded to that particular whistle.

There were times that mom and dad wanted to go into town. If I didn't respond quickly enough I might be left at home by myself. That never happened but there were a couple of times I had to run down the drive way to catch up with the car.

To this day I don't know if they would have left without me. I sure responded quickly after having had it almost happened a couple of times.

My father was the gentlest person I have ever known in my whole life. If only I could have the opportunity to live my life again, I would pay more attention to my father and hope to be more like him.

To all of the young people of the world, love your parents and listen to them. One day you will not have them and you will wish them to be back in your lives. Oh, to hear their voice and to listen to their advice!

Beware; the day comes when they are gone! Afterward there is no going back. If it were possible I would have done it long ago.

DAD'S WORK BENCH

After the new barn was completed, Dad built tool cribs in the corners at the rear of the barn. No one today calls then cribs anymore, but that is what Dad called it and so I did too.

Next to the tool crib in the right rear corner of the barn Dad built a tool bench. I can't remember much about its length and depth. I know it was higher than my head when it was completed.

On the left end of the bench Dad mounted a large vise. He could clamp whatever he was working on in the vise and hold it steady.

I wanted to cut some boards, for what I can't remember, but I climbed up the end of the bench and stood on the work area. Clamping the board in the vise I proceeded to cut the board with Dad's handsaw.

One day I was up on the bench working away when one of my uncles came into the barn and saw me working away cutting a board. He stepped quickly outside and yelled for everyone to come see what I was doing.

I wasn't doing any thing wrong. I was not making a mess. Nor was I breaking any of Dad's tools. Why all the fuss?

Pretty soon several people were in the barn watching me cut my boards. As soon as I had completed my work I climbed down. Everyone was watching me as if they could not believe that a six year old climbed up on the workbench to saw some boards.

What I finally realized was the fact that although I wasn't tall enough to stand on the ground and complete my work, I did the next best thing, I climbed up the end of the bench and now I could get to what I wanted to cut. Many years later I stood at that same workbench and could accomplish whatever task I undertook. I was very proud that

I did not let size stop me. Dad was proud that I would find a way to accomplish a task.

That day when attention was drawn to me I was somewhat taken back. Today I look upon those events as, never let any thing stop you if you really want to accomplish a task.

This has proven true in my adult life as well. There is always a way!

DEAD WAGON

Just saying the words brings back memories of when I was a very young boy. We moved to the farm with a busy highway, which our land fronted and there were events that called for the dead wagon.

No, it was not to retrieve a dead human; rather it was to remove an animal that had been killed on or near the highway.

One time a horse had escaped from its owners pasture and wondered upon the highway until it was directly in front of our property. My sis and I were playing in our back yard when we heard the screech of car tires squealing on the highway and a loud thump.

For some reason the horse decided it wanted to cross the highway directly in front of a car. That is why the sounds of tire squealing were so loud. Needless to say the car hit the horse broadside. The horse rolled up on top of the car.

The horse was injured very badly. Legs were broken and the horse could not move. The horse was in a lot of pain. A policeman arrived shortly after the accident.

Upon checking the animal the policeman decided that it would be best to put the animal out of its misery. Pulling out his revolver he quickly shot the animal right between the eyes. The horse died quickly there beside the highway.

I heard someone ask what would be done with the dead animal. The policeman replied that he had called the dead wagon. I had never heard that term used before.

Soon a large truck arrived and the carcass was drawn up into the truck by a cable.

Many times, after that an animal would escape and be killed on the highway. Always the dead wagon would appear and remove the dead animal.

What and where the body was disposed of, I do not know. I heard it bandied about that the carcass was taken to a grease factory. To this day I do not know if that was true or not

FIVE WHITE SQUIRRELS

Oh the joy of an afternoon, being out in the woods! I had traveled down the road beside Grandma Cora's house. Turning left at the fork in the road I soon was slipping quietly along following the little creek that ran through the left side of the farm's forest. Following a cow path I am moving quietly and very slowly.

This was more of an afternoon of just being out in nature's paradise than to really hunt anything. I did have my trusty shotgun but I really didn't intend to shoot at anything.

Moving my feet slowly, so as to not even make a leaf crumble. I had been in the woods for over half an hour and searching each side of the creek. I was straining to hear or see anything that might be in the trees or on the ground.

So far nothing that would even resemble a squirrel. Not even a leaf moving, only the birds floating from tree to tree. Still it was not a bad day. I simply enjoyed being out in the woods.

Wait! Did I see something move about fifty or sixty feet ahead of me. Yes I did! That is a squirrel moving up the tree trunk. Daring hardly to move, there is little to hide my movements.

Wait a minute there is another one higher up in the tree. Yes, there is! Now I am moving even more slowly. Knees bent and slowly, ever so slowly I creep forward.

One of the squirrels is coming down the tree! Wait a minute, that squirrel is as white as the pure driven snow. The second one is too. Is what?? It is as white as the first one! They are not gathering food. They are just having fun going up and down the tree.

Well I had never seen anything like this. Two white squirrels just having fun with each other as if they were playing a game of hide and seek.

Whoa now, there is a third squirrel! Smaller than the other two, but they were just as white. I decide to sit down and just watch the white squirrel family play around in the tree.

Soon two even smaller squirrels are in the game. Up and down that tree! Out on a limb and then they fly back to the main tree trunk.

I can't believe my eyes! White squirrels everywhere! I decide to lay the shotgun down and just watch the fun they were having. No way would I ever shoot a "WHITE SQUIRREL". Just as the gun touched the ground there was a small noise made by a small stray leaf.

When I raised my eyes to catch a glimpse of the squirrels again there was not one in sight "Nothing"!! I sat there for another half hour but the white squirrels were gone. Where, I have not an idea?

Though I went back to that same tree day after day for a week, I never saw the family of white squirrels ever again.

As a Child

As a child it seems like life goes on forever. Days are so long and time passes so slowly. Oh for those days again when there were no worries, no concerns, except for eating and sleeping.

Even as a teenager I was anxious to be older. To drive a car! To be out of school! Wanting a job! Earn money to buy what, I really did not know. Every fact of life requires money.

Later to want to be a part of a great effort to set the world on fire!! To be known and praised!!

A time of comfort to realize that I'd never achieve greatness! Not even a little flame. But, who cares?

Now as the days slip by faster and faster I want to set the clock back, to slow down time. Once it was only the quickness of minutes. Those followed by quickness of days, until now it is the years that flow as water.

Stop the passage of time, for it flows all too quickly now. When once I was but a small child, now the reference of old has me in its grasp.

Some, when asked if they would like to live life over again respond with a quick 'NO' and bitter smile upon their lips.

No! So say I, for I would live it again and again until I have finally got it right. As many trips as possible, even if I had to start afresh each time!

But it is no use, wish as I may; there is no turning back, no repeats that is known. For the days flow so swiftly. Now I know the dread. For it is coming and none are prepared!

HOG HEAD SOUSE

After the different cuts of the hog meat had been placed in the smoke house I happened to walk into the kitchen where mother was working. Looking to see what was in the dishpan sitting on the stove, was I ever surprised!! There sits the whole complete hogs head.

Snout, sticking straight up in the air! There was some liquid in the pan but I was more interested in what and how the head was to be cooked.

Mother explained that it would require several hours cooking before the meat could be stripped from the bones. As it turned out there was a whole lot of cooking before removing the meat. It seemed like days before mother started taking the meat off the bones.

She used two forks and was removing the outer skin and putting it in another pot. What ever happened to the skin I do not know! Mother continued with the ears, snout, neck and wherever there was some meat.

Soon the jawbone came out. Next the skull was removed and set aside to give to the dogs.

Mother then started tearing apart all of the large pieces of meat. Soon it was a sea of swimming meat in the pan. Seasoning was added including salt and pepper.

Note: the follow recipe was found on the Web:

Cook hog head and ears well done, pull meat off bones, mash fine. Add salt to taste, 1 1/2 cups vinegar, red, black pepper and sage to taste. Refrigerate overnight.

NEW HOUSE

In 1946, a man by the last name of Wright asked Dad if he would sell the farm. I do not know what the selling price was per acre. I do not know if it was ever discussed in front of me. An agreement was reached for Dad to keep one half acre in the southeast corner of the farm, the area where the coal chute was located and closest to Hwy 37.

The coal chute was dismantled and hauled away during the winter. In early 1947, a large bulldozer arrived early one morning before I left for school. Dad did not go to work that day.

Dad had since quit his job at the Monroe Count Airport and was now working at the RCA plant in Bloomington. When I arrived home from school that afternoon the basement was dug. Dad and someone else were digging the footer trenches for the foundation of the house.

The next evening upon arriving home from school the concrete footers had been poured. The following weekend, Lowell Johnson and his son were to start laying the concrete blocks for the basement walls.

At this time we were living in the garage building where Dad had once used to repair cars. When Dad sold the farm, it was with the agreement that we would move soon. I do not know how long we had before moving. I just remember it was in a month or so.

The following Saturday, Dad and I were up very early. Preparations had already been made to have several men there to help. Concrete blocks were delivered as well as cement and sand.

Mr. Johnson's son, John would do the actual setting of the blocks. Three or four people including Dad and myself were to keep concrete blocks at hand so John did not have to take an extra step to reach a block. Another task was to keep the scaffling built up inside the walls.

I was to keep the cement mixed at all times and carried to where John was working. This does not sound difficult, that is until you have been at it for several hours.

There was a mixing box in which the sand and cement was shoveled in measured proportions. The box was six feet long and three feet wide. The sides were about eight to ten inches high.

Three shovels of sand to one shovel of cement were added to the box. I do not remember how much sand and cement was put into the box but it was almost full. The final ingredient needed was water.

I cannot remember but I think Dad had the well drilled before construction of the house began. I remember helping dad install the pipe into the well and setting up the pump.

It was difficult to handle a twenty-foot long two-inch pipe. Dad placed the 29 Model A truck close to the well hole. He chained several two by eight boards across the top of the dump bed. I would be up on the scaffling and Dad would lift the pipe up to me and I helped raise it to the vertical position. Dad would handle the bottom end and tell me which way to move the pipe to get it lined up to get the threads started. Actually the first one was a bit easier because it had the pump mounted on the end.

It was difficult to keep the pipe from free falling into the well pipe. The well was over one hundred and thirty feet deep. If the pipe were dropped into the hole, there would be no way to retrieve it. A new well would have to be dug.

Dad was very careful that he would not lose the pipe. A chain was always wrapped around twice and then hooked back onto the main chain. The chain would bind on the pipe tightly where the pipe could not slip out. This was the safety chain.

To raise or lower the pipe, Dad had two tools that were made to fit the pipe. The handle was about three feet long. The tool somewhat resembled an F. The two arms forming the F were about four inches long. The spacing between them was slightly greater than the diameter of the pipe.

Once the pipe was placed between the arms, if the outer end of the handle was raised, it would bind enough of the pipe so it could be used to raise or lower the pipe. Two of these tools were used.

When the first pipe end was protruding from the well casing about two feet, it was time to prepare another pipe to be joined to it.

Since the water was to be pumped from a depth of greater than one hundred feet, the rod that actually worked the pump was changed to a wooden one. Normally a metal rod is used and it is about a half inch in diameter.

This wooden rod had to be inside the two-inch pipe. The rods had to be screwed together as well. We worked more than five hours installing the pipes and rods in the well.

I do not remember if we carried water from neighbor, Lorrie Heltonburg's house or not. She lived directly across the gravel road from our new house.

Now back to the cement mixture, water is added to the sand and cement slowly, because if too much is added, the mixture will be too soupy. Since the mixing box was close to being full already, adding more sand and gravel would make it all the more difficult to mix, without splashing it out over the sides.

A large cement hoe is used to combine the ingredients. It certainly was much more difficult to do than I believed. A batch had to be mixed as quickly as possible so the block layer would not have to stand and wait.

Block laying started just after seven o'clock in the morning. No breaks were taken. There was no time taken to eat lunch. Six o'clock that evening, the last block was laid. John Johnson, in his early twenty's, laid over twelve hundred blocks that day. Lowell was very proud of his son, as any father would have been.

Everyone was tired that evening. Tiredness was soon diminished by the thoughts that our new house was finally under construction.

The basement walls were allowed to cure for several days. The following Saturday, work began on the floor joists. Lowell, his son John, Dad and I worked on the flooring and built stud walls to frame the house.

Plywood was not yet used in housing construction. All of the exterior walls including the roof were covered with six-inch wide boards. They were nailed at each stud with three nails. This does not sound like a lot, but let me tell you, it takes a long time when you are doing it with a hammer. It took several days to do just the exterior walls.

There is so much involved in the construction of a house. It would take hundreds of pages to describe every step. I'll conclude by saying the house was finished within six months. We were happy to move into our new home, I was around sixteen at the time. I didn't get to live there long as I joined the navy soon after graduating from High School, but I was happy that I had a bedroom upstairs.

Parts Washer/Killing Ants

How do these two names fit together? It's not what you think if you have been raised in the country. Well it takes more than that really. Take a young man of eleven years and give him the task of cleaning dirty parts off an automobile engine.

That was my job as I was to scrape the dirt, muck, grease soaked dirt and just about any thing else you would want to throw in. Anyway that was my job.

My cleaning station if it can be called that was just outside the large door of the garage. There was more than enough drive way, that a vehicle could be parked on the north side of the garage. It was an area about twelve feet wide that served several purposes.

I had brought out the oil pan and several other parts that were caked with oil and dirt. I went about scraping each piece carefully and not to miss any spots. Next, came a washing of the parts with gasoline, using an old paintbrush.

Working slowly, because I had no certain time that the parts had to be cleaned. My attention was drawn to an anthill coming up out of the ground right where the slope begins to drop off over the hillside. Be a devout hater of ants, I took the paintbrush and let some gas drop down into the hole where the ants were coming and going.

Doing this several times did not seem to deter the ant's one bit. Maybe a few were killed if the gas droplets happened to fall directly on them. I know what I will do; I will pour some gas into their hole, and then set it on fire.

Going into the garage I soon returned with a box of kitchen matches. Slowly, I took out a match and struck it against the side of the box. It instantly bursts into the bright yellow.

Standing about three feet from the ant hole, I tossed the lighted match toward the gasoline-saturated dirt. I missed, and the flame went out. Once again I got another match, striking it and waited for the wood to catch fire. I am more careful this time to toss the match directly on the gasoline soaked soil. It bursts into a small flame but did not burn long. The gasoline had evaporated and didn't leave much fuel to burn off.

Waiting for the flame to be completely out I poured more gas into the ant hole. This time I wasted no time in getting a match going and tossed on the gasoline. I really got a good high flame this time, about three feet high. It flamed for a couple of minutes then soon burned out.

Inspecting the ant hole it was completely black. Not an ant in sight! Not even one little body. Gone, burned up I guess!

This same procedure was used many times. I soon ridded the hill side of any ants. I don't ever remember ants ever starting a new colony on the bank again.

I watched for them. I looked and looked but they never came back. I guess it was really due to the residue that remained in the soil after the fire had died away. The whole bank smelled of grease and gasoline for a long time afterward. So much for keeping the earth clean and healthy. At that point in time there wasn't any talk about keeping the environment clean.

POOR AND DIDN'T KNOW IT!

Growing up in southern Indiana my family didn't have much but we got along back during and after the depression years that hit in the 30's. I never missed a meal and never went to bed hungry. I may not have had the best of clothes but I always had clothes and had shoes to wear.

When I was in the first grade of school it was evident that many of the children came from a home with less then my family had.

There was a young girl in the class that wore dresses made from flour sacks or maybe it was bran sacks. It was evident her family was poor.

Some girls in the class were making fun of her dress. The teacher quickly put a stop to their teasing. I felt sorry but I could do nothing.

My family always had an automobile. Dad also had his big truck, a ton and half Ford. One of the people Dad hired to deliver coal stuck a potato on the exhaust pipe. (A relative did this but I don't remember who,) This produced a whistling sound but was not good for the engine. Dad had to overhaul the engine due to their practical joke. Soon after we moved to the ten-acre farm Dad and bought a 1929 Model A truck.

Our house was nothing fancy, three rooms and a lean-to where I slept during our first years there. We did not have running water in the house, but we did have running water of sorts. If the bucket became low or empty of water, Mom would say "run out and get a bucket of water". So, we did have running water. We just did not have the kind that is normally accepted with the statement of running water.

We did not have a refrigerator when we moved to the farm. Instead we had an icebox, which was replenished twice a week with ice. I cannot remember what days of the week, ice was delivered.

However it was not long before Dad bought an electric refrigerator. We got to have ice cubes and everything that needed refrigeration was inside. There was no such thing as a frost-free refrigerator back then. From time to time the freezer had to have the frost and ice removed. What Dad did not tell mother was to not use a sharp pointed knife to remove ice.

Mother cut through one of the coils inside the freezer. I cannot remember the words exchanged but there was sorta a shouting match between the two of them. Dad had to solder the injured coil. Next he had to learn how to recharge the cooling system.

At that time refrigerators used ammonia gas for the cooling agent. It sure was a mess and one can not stay nearby when the fumes are in the area. We knew from first hand experience.

Dad completed the repairs of the refrigerator and every thing got back to normal. Suffice it to say there were no more sharp objects used to remove the frost and ice that accumulates on the coils.

We always had food to eat. I never went to bed hungry. All of this was due to, Dad's planning and foresight. We always had pork to eat. From pork chops, to chicken. We had very little beef owing to the fact that the cow had a calf each year and the calf was sold as soon as it was weaned. I guess it brought in more money for other things. Many times I would have to take the calf to a different part of the farm to let it graze.

More than once that calf decided that it wanted to go in a direction other than what I wanted to go. The rope tied to the calf's halter and me on the other end. Many times the calf would take off at a fast gallop dragging me behind it. I had many rope burns on my hands because I was too dumb to turn loose of the rope and let the calf go where ever it wanted to go. Still I was always sad when the truck came to take the calf to the auction or to the packing house.

I have related the story about raising chickens. I grew to dislike chicken.

To this day I do not eat much chicken. I get the smell of cleaning chickens back when I am close to a piece of chicken. Can you tell that I don't like chicken to this day?

I remember that my Dad stopped at the county trustee's office. The trustee was giving folks with little money a chit to get a free bag of beans. Dad had gone to the trustee's office to try to get dried beans for his family. In just a short time Dad came back to the car and he was really upset. The trustee said Dad made too much money and refused to give him the chit. Dad fairly jumped in the car and I will never forget his words. "I will never beg again to get food from anyone. To the day he died he never asked for free food again. Dad was a very proud man.

Dad and Mom were very frugal with their money. Still they bought what was needed. As far as I know they never bought any thing if they could not pay cash for it. The only exception I can think of is when they purchased the ten acre farm.

I am not really sure if in fact they borrowed money. I remember the day that Dad was to pay the man he purchased the farm from. Dad asked me to look and he had ten one hundred dollar bills, which he placed in my hand.

I didn't know what a dollar bill looked like, let alone a one hundred dollar bill. I was so proud that Dad let me hold the money for a short time.

Dad always had cash money to pay for a load of coal when he went to coal mine. He always had cash money when he purchased an automobile.

The only exception to that was when I had just graduated from high school I wanted to buy my own car. I didn't have any money but still wanted my own car. I was working at the Graham Ford motor company and they had a used, very used, 1939 two-door sedan Chevy for sale. I told Dad and asked him to look at it before I actually made a down payment.

Dad never told me that I couldn't buy it but the next day Dad came to the dealership and purposed that he trade in his car on a brand new Ford coupe. It was a two-door sedan and was the prettiest blue color. Dad's only comment was that the car belonged to me and I had to make the payments on it. The car was purchased in Dad's name, so I only had the bragging rights to ownership of the car.

I joined the Navy two months after that and the car reverted to Dad.

I would not be making enough money in the navy to even think about making the car payment. I made sixty eight dollars a month during those first months of my navy career.

Back to being poor and didn't know it. I always got a new pair of shoes each year. There were two pairs of bib overalls. Don't remember if there were new shirts or not. I always had clothes to wear and a jacket for winter wear.

As I grew older there were more demands for looking proper at school.

It seemed that I was the average guy in dress and demeanor.

The only exception was during the senior year. The guys had cream-colored cord pants. We put just about every name of our classmates on them. Of course, ones girl friend's name had to be prominent on the front somewhere.

So we were not really dirt poor but we were not rich. I had a good life and enjoyed every day of living on the ten acre farm.

Slaying the Chigger
Weed Knights

The family needed milk. I liked milk with my morning cereal. There was always a need for milk in our home. Mother's cooking and for just plain drinking. We needed a milk cow.

Dad bought a milk cow. A mean spirited one. She was mean to everyone that went into the cow pasture. That is except for Dad and Mom. Mother could get that cow to do anything she wanted. Move over a foot and the cow moved. Move ahead and the cow moved forward.

When one of us kids went into the cow pasture that cow was sure to look up and come running if she was near by. Kids would fly for the fence and roll under the bottom string of barbed wire. We hustled in a hurry.

Do you think that cow would come to the barn when it was time for milking? NO! I do not know what happened in the morning when I was still in bed asleep. But it soon became my duty to go after the cow for the evening milking, even when there was always a fresh mix of grain and hay for her to eat.

Up over the hill and I would look around the open field. Cow could not be seen but I knew just where to look for her! She had a favorite place to lay during the late afternoon hour, so off I would go to reach the far back part of the area behind Grandma Cora's house.

Chigger weeds are thick in the meadow and growing about knee high, just the right height to impart a new crop of chiggers. I do not know why chiggers like these weeds but they do. It is always best to stay on the beaten path so as not to garner a new batch of chiggers.

Just as I topped the hill behind the new barn, I picked up a small slim board, about three feet long, inch and half wide and quarter of an inch thick. Actually it was an old lath board, which is used on walls when plastering a house wall. I do not know where this one came from but it fit right in, in my plan to slay the knights of the chigger weed and their evil prince the leader of the blackberry gang that lived in the blackberry bushes behind Grandma Cora's garden.

Soon I was swinging my newly selected sword and cutting off the heads of those knights closest to the edge of the path I was traveling. A mighty swing to the left and the heads rolled right off of the chigger weed knights. Another mighty swing from left to right and I beheaded at least half a dozen more knights. Soon I was swinging quickly as my pace quickened. Soon I was running as I swung my mighty sword. Left, right, right, left!

Almost at a run I depart the open field of the chigger week knights. Breathing deeply and slowing the pace I head right to the spot where our old milk cow lay contently chewing her cud. Swinging her head to look right at me but not budging an inch. I had to resort to picking up a fallen branch and tapping her gently on the hind quarters so as to convince her to get up and head for the barn.

The cow and I had to depart the blackberry patch at the same gate I went through on my way in. Old Guernsey was in no hurry. She was walking her slow walk along the path where I had just slain at least a hundred of the chigger week knights. I knew they would be waiting for me and I could not get that cow to go any faster than her slow pace.

Now I had to defend my self against the chigger weed knights even more diligently than I had on my way in. I knew they would try to surround me. They would slip around behind and give me a nasty blow, but even with the slow pace we soon left the field behind and was at the barn. The cow turning to gave me a look as if "I'll get even with you tomorrow."

That cow had a look in her eye that is hard to forget. I knew that she would hide even deeper in the Blackberry Gang's home turf. Tomorrow I would sharpen the edge of my sword so as to more easily behead the evil chigger weed knights.

Tomorrow another day in the fight against the evil of the world where good over comes the dastardly thugs that try to reach the one that can save others.

THE FIRST NEW HOUSE
THAT WAS NEVER BUILT

Sometime during 1938 or 1939, mother and dad decided to build a new house. I vaguely remember discussion about it, as I was only about six or seven. One day we went down the hill into the field south of the present two-room house we were living in. It was at this place that Mother and Dad decided they wanted the new house built.

Later, we stood in the field along side a sapling and Dad put stakes in the ground to mark where the corners of the house would be. As I recall, Dad did not use a tape measure or anything, but stepped it off to determine distance.

The layout of the house seemed very large at that time. This of course had to do with the small house we were presently living in. By the standards of today, the new house would have seemed small as well. There was to be a basement to the new house. We were going to have a house with a basement!! Wonder of wonders!! Very few people could afford to build during the 1930's and they sure did not have enough money to put a basement under their house.

I remember the new windows and window casing as well as the new doors and door casing were hauled in and stored in the hayloft of the barn. There was oak flooring stored away as well. The hayloft was half-full of all the new things for the house. I assume Mother and Dad bought as they could afford. All of the doors, windows, casings and oak flooring were eventually used in the new house, which was built in 1947 and is still occupied by owners that bought it from Mother in 1968-69.

In the summer of 1941, trucks with concrete blocks showed up. There must have been thousands of them. (Later I learned there was about 800 blocks.) From a kid's eye, it seemed like a lot more. They were stacked just to the south of the existing house, in the cow pasture.

This was an opportunity for a kid. The stacks were much higher than my head but the blocks formed steps up to the very top of the pile. Soon I was on top of the highest pile, standing there to survey my kingdom and the world. Up here I could see all the way to the top of the hill in back of the barn and down to the gravel road that led to our house.

The new house was to be constructed in the summer of 1942. World War II started December 7, 1941 and Mother and Dad's house would never be constructed as they had planned. After a long postponement, Dad began making plans in 1946 for a new home in the southeast corner of the property. He sold 9 ½ acres of his property and kept ½ acre for the new home site.

Going back to the spring of 1941, work had started on digging the basement of the house. I don't think that I drove the truck during the initial runs.

I believe that mother drove the truck and dad operated the hand dirt slip behind the truck. The dirt slip is about 40 inches wide. It has handles on each side and is about twelve inches deep. From front to back it was about 30 inches.

Two horses normally pulled this device. I have seen horses pull similar slips full of dirt. It ass all they could do to pull when it is being loaded or digging. After it was full, horses did not have a difficult time moving it.

Back to our situation, Mother drove the truck and dad operated the dirt slip. When dad was controlling the slip he wanted mother to put the truck in double low or as we called it granny gear. The truck engine speed would be brought up to about 600 to 800 rpm. This was pretty slow. That way if dad hit a rock or root, he had complete control and would not be hurt.

The driver of the truck however must lean to the left out the doorway; turn your head as far to the left as possible to see Dad. After the slip was filled, Dad would step to the side and run up to the side of the truck and step on the running board. He would ride there until approaching the place he wanted to dump the dirt.

In this case we were taking the dirt completely to the corner where the gravel road turned off Highway 37. This was the southeast corner of Dad's property. I did not know it then but he had plans to build a garage there some day. At this time, all I knew was, we were filling in the corner.

I do not remember the details but I had learned to drive the 29 Model A truck. Now I am sitting in the driver's seat and leaning left, out the open door. Sometime earlier the door had been completely removed, probably for the very reason that it made it more difficult to look back toward the rear of the truck for an extended period of time if the door was in the way.

I had made several runs with the slip full of dirt. Boy, I thought I was getting good at this!! Dad did not have to worry when he had a man to drive for him!!! Wonderful, I could do what I had seen others do!!! I could run that truck so expertly that I was probably better than anyone Dad had ever had. Why I could drive that truck right up to within a nits eyebrow of any tree, stump, drop-off, building or anything that got in my way! I was the best of the world drivers! That's why my Dad allowed me to drive for him!!!

We worked on the basement about every evening. Dad would come home from work and off we would go, me driving with him doing the easy stuff!

As we circled back from emptying the slip Dad stepped off and waited as I slowly approached into the scooped out area. Dad would always give me directions as to where I was to place the truck so he could keep an even bottom to the digging.

Ok, slow down, double clutch, so the transmission can be shifted down into Granny! It was extremely difficult to do this and not grind the gears. They were straight cut gears and almost everyone had to come to a complete stop before going into Granny gear.

Being the complete expert, I had learned to double clutch! That is, to press the clutch in and move the gearshift to the neutral position. The clutch was released and immediately pressed back in to help get the gears so they were moving at the same speed. At that time the gearshift was moved into the granny position.

I had double clutched down to Granny and the truck had not come to a complete stop. Boy was my neck tired from craning around to see Dad! So, just this once I did not look back but kept the truck moving along ever so slowly. I was sure dad handled the dirt slip with no problem.

I was looking straight ahead, in my revelry. The superb driver was in complete control. SUDDENLY, THERE IS DAD!!!! Walking right beside the truck!! No way!! He is supposed to be behind operating the dirt slip. Well, there he is and he is saying things to me that I did not want to hear. No—make him say the things that I wanted to hear!! "Keep your mind on what you are doing. Don't daydream but PAY ATTENTION," is what I heard.

"Now circle back and watch me," he said. Those were words that were said coolly, calmly and without any rise in the tone of his voice. Those words were deadly to me. Fear ran up my backbone, like a broad yellow stripe. There I was congratulating myself on what a fine driver that I was and "I SCREWED UP".

There are no other words to describe it. I sank down in the seat and put my mind into high gear. I WOULD WATCH, I WOULD LISTEN, AND I WOULD LOOK BACK. I don't have to be told twice that I had made a mistake.

Dad and I made many passes through the basement diggings that summer and fall. I was a pro and I was going to prove it to my father. I never missed looking back nor did I ever have to be reprimanded ever again for not paying attention.

Dad had a way of talking slowly, calmly and getting his point across. I never saw him angry at anything or anyone, but I tell you he could get his point across to a person and—well you understood!! There were many times in my life that I had to come and stand before my dad for a verbal reprimand.

I used to say "I would rather have him whip me than have to stand there and listen to him, answer his questions and ADMIT THAT I WAS WRONG".

He was the best Dad that a boy could ever have had!!!!!!!!!!!!

THE TREATMENT OF A CUT FOOT

Empty canning fruit jars were stored upside down by the peach tree located inside the garden fence. It was my job to carry the jars and place them under the peach tree. I had done this hundreds of times, maybe a thousand times or more, or so it seemed to this young lad.

One day I happened to be in the garden and around the peach tree. I don't remember how old I was then, maybe ten or so years old. What was about to happen, seems surreal now.

There I was paying attention to what I was doing. Was I really? I have no idea what or why.

Suddenly I felt a sharp pain my left foot. Looking down I see blood on the ground and there is a steady stream from my foot to the puddle on the ground. I had stepped upon the broken bottom of a fruit jar. How and why it was broken I have no idea. Still I had found it with my foot.

During the summer months most kids did not wear shoes. As soon as May came, off would come the shoes. We neighborhood kids could not wait to get rid of those shoes.

This day there is no one home at my house. Mother and Dad were both working. What am I to do? Why go to Grandmother Cora's house, of course! That was the only logical solution to my problem. Good ole Grandma!!

Off I go hobbling toward Grandmother Cora's house. Hurrying as fast as I dared go and not wanting to get dirt in the cut, which was right in the instep. With left heel down and right foot going, as fast as it dared, I knew I needed help quickly.

Soon, I was at Grandmother's house and through her kitchen door, which was the back door of the house. Grandmother Cora listens to my story and them tells me to go outside and she will be with me in a minute.

It seems like ten forevers before she stepped out of the house with a pan in one hand and the kerosene bucket in the other. I was directed to sit down, which I did. Next, I was to put my injured foot in the pan, Then, she proceeded to pour kerosene on top of my foot until it came above the cut. I don't mean to give you the idea that it didn't hurt. It burned like fire. What kept my foot in that pan was Grandmother Cora's hand! She was pressing my foot into the pan and I for sure was not strong enough to move with her hand holding my leg still.

Again we must have set there at least ten forevers before she would allow me to remove my foot from the pan.

Finally the pain subsided but I sure did not put my foot on the ground. I sure did not want to get dirt in the cut and I was sure it would start hurting again if I put any weight on my left foot.

I don't remember any bandages or any thing else being done to my foot. It healed quickly. I was soon walking on it with no thought to keeping dirt out of the cut.

I don't know what the kerosene did in the cut. I don't know what kind of healing power there was. All I know is, it did not require a trip to the doctor's office. Which would have required a wait until one of my parents came home.

I am sure I told my parents when they came home. I'm sure mother looked at the cut but can't remember what was said.

Needless to say I never went under the peach tree again unless I had shoes on. I was not going to risk getting another bad cut.

Beans, Bacon
And
Poke Greens

I just loved to wake up in the morning when Mom was cooking. The houses smelled so good, besides the kitchen was always warm. I really loved the aroma when she was cooking bacon. The smell was almost more than I could stand. Standing up beside my bed I was almost standing in front of the kitchen stove. I could see what was being cooked.

Dad liked pork chops and had them frequently for breakfast. To go with the pork chops there would always be gravy. To this day I love to have what is called white gravy. Take a home made biscuit and crumble it up in the plate. Over this add three or four large scopes of gravy. It would make a meal in its self. Throw in a well browned pork chop and there is no finer meal. I could eat that meal four or five times a day as a child.

I liked going with mother when she went to the smoke shed. She would have long decided what cut of meat she was going after. I think my favorite was the slabs of bacon. First she would take the meat down and lay it flat. She brought the big sharp kitchen knife she was particular to. Mom carefully unwraps the meat. Laying the pins in a neat little pile. Laying back the layers of cloth and then the paper the meat was wrapped in.

This is where the sharp knife really was used. Mon could cut the straightest line down the slab of bacon. She always used two cut for each slice of meat. After cutting as many slices of bacon she wanted then it was time to turn the knife sideways and make a cut to separate the bacon from the skin.

The skin was never wasted. It had another delightful pot it would wind up in. My Grandmother Cora would slice the skin into strips about a quarter of an inch wide which she placed into the pot of white navy beans she had on the stove cooking. This gave the beans the bestest flavor. Now we kids didn't have much use for the cooked skin. It was however a favorite of all the adults that ate at her house. Grandma always cooked her beans with lots of water. The water took on the flavor of the beans and bacon skin. It was one of the best meals I ever had at her house.

When it was time to have a meal of beans, a regular plate was used. The beans and the juice as I will call it are dipped directly into the plate. It was at this time that I was introduced to catsup. A liberal amount of it was put into the plate as well. Next corn bread was crumbled into the plate. A spoon is used to gather all of the wonderful soup and beans. I know I would have several plate full's before getting up from the table.

There is not a finer meal. Even today when grandkids come to our house, they have to have beans with a special of Grandpa's fried potatoes. I don't fix them any different than any other cook. What I do however, is leave the potatoes undisturbed in the pan until they are golden brown on the bottom. Turning them over and then adding slices of a medium sized onion. The onions are pushed into the cooking oil so they will add their flavor to the whole skillet of golden brown potatoes. This seems to be the manner that most of the adults in the family like their potatoes as well. When we have this meal there are always two pots of beans. One white and normally pinto beans so there are two chooses to add to the meal.

Going back to Grandma Cora's house I don't even remember any other meal at her house other than greens. Why do I remember the greens? You would too if you had to go help pick the greens. I mean we are not talking store bough ten greens. We are not talking about greens that were grown in the garden. I mean the kind of greens that were picked along side the gravel road that run in front of her house.

When Grandma said it was time to pick greens we kids knew what she was talking about. There was poke which is a sorta large leafy plant.

Only the tenderest top of the poke chute was to be collected. She did take the small leaves on the stem and put them in the collection. Next were the dandelions. Once again only the tenderest parts from the center of the plant was collected. There were many other green leafy plants gathered but I cannot remember the names.

The poke shoots were stripped of their leaves which went into the greens. The stalk was washed and then cut into pieces about two to three inches long. Now it was cut into half the long way. This gave two pieces. After all the pieces are cut, then they are washed. This is the really great part of the preparation. The poke is dipped into a mixture of beaten eggs, salt, a smidgen of sugar, a touch of black pepper. After this bath it is rolled in white flour.

It is ready to be placed into the hot frying pan. There is a goodly bit of bacon grease in the pan. The battered poke is gently laid into frying pan. Little bubbles come up around the pieces of poke. As each piece browns it is turned over to be browned on the other side. We kids would almost fight to get a piece of the poke. It had a wonderful hint of bacon as each piece was chewed. I know there was never any left to be placed on the dinner table. I ate my share and then some. I would eat it again today if it was prepared like Grandma Cora fixed it.

I doubt there are any kids of today that would even try a bite of poke. Thinking, if it didn't come out of the grocery store that it is not to be eaten. They do not know what they are missing. The children of today do not know what they are missing. If only I could go back and stand beside grandma and eat those poke stems again.

BEE TREE

What in the world is a bee tree? Why is it called a bee tree? Where do you find a bee tree? But I am getting ahead of the story and what it entails.

It was a beautiful bright late spring day! The sun was shining brightly! The weather was just right, not too hot but at the same time it was not too cold either. We were playing, doing what, I don't remember now but I am sure we were busy doing whatever it is that kids do when they don't have to go to school. Chores are done and the rest of the day is to do whatever it is we use to while away the time.

I am twelve years old and I had already read all of the books that I had checked out from the traveling bookmobile. Five books and I had gone through every last one of them. Now it is time to let the mind wonder and see what it can come up with. My sis and I were in our front yard, not really doing anything but at the same time we were whiling away the morning hours.

Who should walk up the bank beside the highway but our first cousin, Richard? He had a twenty two rifle slung over his shoulder. Of course we were happy to see him. Did not get to see him very much since he lives on Chapel Hill. This is over twenty miles by the road. Richard informed me that he had cut across country and it was a lot shorter that way.

Inquiring as to what he was doing in our 'neck of the woods' he said he was out squirrel hunting and decided to walk to our house. This is almost unheard of a kid of twelve years of age and out hiking cross country. Much less it was still morning so he must have started out very early. We invited him in for a drink of water and inquired if he was hungry? No he replied and pulled out a bisket and said he was just fine. One thing leads to another and soon we were talking about his ability to hit a squirrel with a twenty two rifle. To my surprise he told me he did not shot at a squirrel unless he could get a head shot. Wow, a head shot. I couldn't hit a squirrel with a rifle unless he was sitting on the barrel of the gun.

I must interject here that Richard is the next to youngest son of my dad's oldest brother. Vernie is actually dad's half brother, he had a different father than dad. Vernie did not have a good reputation; he was known as a gambler and would do any thing to win at the game of poker. It is reputed that sometime during his early teen hood that he had killed a man. If this is true or not I do not have idea.

Conversation soon turned to the fact that I didn't believe him. He would have to demonstrate that he was that accurate with the rifle. I had tried using a rifle before but could never hold the gun still enough to sight on the head of the squirrel. I used the old fashion way, a shot gun that had a lot of pellets in each shot, that way I was more assured that I might hit a squirrel.

Richard and I were soon on our way back into the woods behind our farm. In fact we had not gotten to the woods yet but were walking down the road past Grandmother Cora's house when Richard spotted a squirrel high up in a tree. We stopped talking and walked about quietly while Richard was seeking a spot where he could see the head of the squirrel. Ping went the rifle and the squirrel come tumbling out of the tree. Dead as a doorknob. Never even twitched after it hit the ground. Picking up the squirrel I inspected it closely as to determine where the bullet has entered the body. There were no wounds on the body but when I looked at the head it was quite evident that the shot had hit the squirrel in the side of the head. Wow, again not only had Richard said he only did head shots but he had proved it. I was in awe of such accuracy. Soon we were headed back to my house where we cleaned the squirrel and had him tucked neatly in the frig.

Richard stayed over night with us, I don't remember where he was bedded down but I am sure it was a comfortable bed. Relatives were always welcomed and treated with due respect. When I awoke the next morning Richard was gone. Where, I had no idea. I had not heard him get up or leave the house. Since I had no idea where he might be I did what I usually—nothing—nothing that is, I went about entertaining my self.

About ten o'clock Richard comes strolling in from the direction of Grandmother Cora's house. He told me he was getting to know the lay of the land behind our farm. The general area that I had hunted many times. Most times I didn't really want to find a squirrel; rather I roamed the hill sides. I followed the streams of water until I got tired of that and headed back home. It was wonderful to search out the different hills and hollers.

Richard had exciting news. He had noticed a stream of bees coming and going in a particular direction. Their flight took them into the same woods that I had haunted many times. What happen is that I had never thought of following the general direction that the bees were traveling. Undoubtfully the bees were going back to where the bees had made a hive. I had seen bees going and coming from our bee hive. They seemingly knew where the hive is located after they had collected a bunch of pollen from flowers and plants.

What Richard had done was follow the return flight of the bees and discovered that they had entered a "hole" high up in a very large tree. Who knows how long the bees had been using that tree as a hive.

We talked and talked about how we could get to the beehive and rob them of the honey that have stored. That is the same as having a bee hive box in your back yard. The only thing is that the bee hive is placed where it would be convient to take the honey from time to time.

With a domestic bee hive the hives are robbed in late spring so the bees will have time to collect more honey to tide them over the winter months. We had no such compunction. We didn't care where the bees would go if we could rob their storage of honey. Still it was early in the summer season and they would have plenty of time to replenish their store of honey.

But back to the problem we were faced with. The hole the bees were using was not large enough for us to reach our hand inside the hole. Besides what would we do so as not to disturbed the bees while at the same time we would taking their honey. The bees would not like that one little bit. They would come out buzzing and stinging any thing near their entry way. Well we didn't have that problem yet, what was more important at this time was how are we going to get up to the hole in the first place. Our minds worked and worked but could not come up with any workable way to get up to the bee hole.

Next we decided that the tree must be cut down so as to make the bee hole directly available to us. We decided that we would use dad's cross cut saw to cut through the three foot trunk. Soon we had a larger crew to help with the work. Georgia and her brother Gary and David were enlisted to help get all of the equipment needed to cut down the tree.

It was so late in the day that we decided that we would wait until the next morning so as to have more time to cut the tree down. While walking back home it was brought up that my dad had a bee smoker and a bee hat that he used when he was robbing his hive. I knew where all of the items needed were stored. Arriving back at our barn the necessary equipment was collected and ready for our work the next day.

We were all up early and were headed toward the bee tree by nine o'clock. Almost an unheard of time, for a bunch of kids, setting about on their first experience of robbing a bee tree! Arriving at the tree, items were set about in the general areas where they would be needed. The saw was picked up and Richard and I soon had a good cut going about three feet above the ground level. It was slow going as neither he nor I were very good at operating a large two man saw. Still we soon found the rhythm needed and we were making good progress. We stopped often as the work soon brought sweat to our brows. After working for what seemed hours we were ready to make the final few cuts needed to fall the tree. Careful now as we didn't want the tree to fall on us or any of the others that was with us.

Suddenly the tree began to make a groaning sound and then started to lean in the direction we wanted the tree to fall. We had spent a lot of time deciding on just where we wanted the tree to fall. We wanted the bee hole to be on the upper side of the trunk when it was lying on the ground. Our planning paid off and the bee hole was right where we wanted it to be.

The bees were not too happy with the falling of the tree and were coming out in swarms trying to find who had disturbed their hive. We were ready and had the smoker going and soon had dispersed the angry swarm of bees. Where they went we had no idea and didn't care just as long as they stayed away from us. With all our care all of us had received several bee stings. Still we were eager to get on with opening the tree trunk so we could get to the honey inside.

We decided that we would make a cut about two feet above the hole and do the same below the hole. The crosscut saw was way easier to use since we could cut straight across the trunk of the tree. The cut we made was about ten inches deep. Now we had to use the axe as a wedge and drive it into the wood. We finally got one side to split and started on the other side. It seemed like no time at all passed but I am sure that it took longer than we thought as we finally got the trunk split on both sides and it was a simple matter to lift it off. This exposed the entire honey comb. There were areas of a very dark honey in the comb. Higher up there was the bright color of new honey and comb.

We didn't to waste a drop of honey but at the same time all of us take a sample of both colors and declared that it all was the best honey that we had ever tasted. We had planned ahead and had a large number three washing tub that had been scrubbed clean before we left the house. I must tell you that we had a lot of honey. The tub was about three quarters full when we had removed every drop of honey in the cavity inside the tree.

There was a lot of laughing and joking as we took turns carrying the washing tub of honey back home. We had honey in the morning we had honey at noon and of course we had honey at dinner as well.

Robbing the bee tree was the talk of my parents. Details were given as to our plans. The gathering of all the tools needed were covered and noted that all had been cleaned and stored where each one was found. I do not remember a lot of conversation from dad but he had a lot of gentle smiles as each key point was explained.

I have no idea how long the honey lasted. I know I ate a lot of the comb and honey together. I don't remember that any one complained that they had too much honey. In fact we were sad when the supply was finally consumed.

I have not heard of any one else finding a bee tree much less robbing it of the honey it contained. Yet here are four or five kids that not only found the bee tree but claimed the honey it contained. What else can be said of kids and what they can accomplish when they have a motive to accomplish a task? It has always been my motto that if a task can't be accomplished one way, back off and figure out another way to the goal.

If you are worried about the bees, don't. They moved on to a new home and started again to gather honey to feed the workers, the queen bee and the hordes of new bees that would be born to the colony. That is the way it is when a new queen bee is born, she and a bunch of workers bees leave the hive and find a new home for a new colony of life.

Post Script

Richard went into the army as soon as he was able. He was a crack shooter with a rifle and was sent to Korea when the war began. I do not know the details but he was killed by friendly fire when his group stopped at night to rest. A young life snuffed out before he had a chance to learn who he really was. War is terrible! It is a senseless killing of young men to satisfy the whims of old men. Nothing is ever gained by war, except the crippling of and the loss of young lives who will never know what it is to grow old.

CHILDHOOD TELEPHONE

Telephones and being out in the country were not too far from the old tin can phone with a wire stretched between them. In the 1930's all of the phones in our part of the country were on party lines. Ours had from eight to twelve people assigned to our party line.

One long ring and two short ones was our assigned signal that we had a phone call. We could call any one on our party line if we knew their particular ring signal.

If you wanted the operator it was just one long ring. At the Telephone Exchange Office, someone was always there to take our call. The operator would ring a number in town or place a long distance call to other parts of the country.

My childhood fiend Boyd and I were playing one day and decided we would make our own phone line between two tall trees across the road from Grandmother Cora's house. The trees were sugar trees so they were easy to climb to up within five or six feet of the top of the tree.

We found two tin cans that would be our transmitter and receiver. Going through a lot of trash we finally found the right cans. Next we had to have a copper wire long enough to stretch between the two trees.

Dad always had old transformers lying around and we found one with enough wire to reach between the selected trees. Only thing we had to do was unwind the wire from the transformer. This sounds easy until one discovers that the metal framework has to be removed first.

Using a hammer and screwdriver we soon had the laminated metal removed. We had to slowly unwind the wire and keep it in a nice neat coil so we would not have kinks and curls in the wire.

Several hours had passed since we first started building our own telephone service. Climbing into the tree nearest Grandma Cora's house we had no trouble getting the wire up into the tree. What we had not included in the plan was how to get the wire out over the tree branches and the same thing in the second tree.

We used a rock tied to the wire and tossed it out through the upper branches. Could not do that at the second tree. We had to go back to the scrap pile and get another transformer and repeat the same operation as on the first one.

Now, we had to climb the second tree and repeat the rock on the end to get through the upper branches. This accomplished, the two wires were tied together and we slowly pulled the first wire up and into the second tree.

With that completed we now had to have holes in the bottom of the cans to attach the wires. Once again, down the tree and back to Dad's tool shed we go. Selecting the right tool proved difficult, as we needed a sharp pointed tool to make the hole.

Finally, we found an awe. Dad used it for making holes in leather. Surely making four little holes would not dull the awe. We got our holes punched and the tools put away so we proceed back to the trees.

I go up one tree and Boyd goes up the other. Securing the can to the wire was simple. We pushed the wire into one hole and back out the second hole then wrapped the end around the main wire several times. This made a secure connection.

Now, time to check our telephones! Each of us pulled the wire as tight as possible and placed the can to our ears. Nothing! I could not hear one word over my phone, nor could Boyd. Oh no, One of us has to talk and the other listen.

I yell to Boyd to talk to me. He does, but I heard nothing. I yell to him to speak louder. Now he is hollering into the can. It is so loud that I could hear him without benefit of the telephone can!

We tried many more times and finally gave up. We couldn't hear anything over our telephones but we were hoarse from yelling back and forth between the trees.

Did it ever work? I have no idea. I don't think so. It did keep two young boys busy for an entire day to make our tin can telephones and to install them in the trees. Did we ever try it again? I don't remember! I doubt that we ever tried out the new and untrustworthy can telephone system again.

FLYING SHOT GUN

My dad and his brother, Uncle Ethel hunted a lot when we first moved to the farm. I don't remember how old I was when this event happened but I know I had not started school yet. I turned six in March so this story happened when I was five years old. Rabbit hunting season starts in the late fall and goes into the winter. There was no snow on the ground and I remember that I did not have a jacket on.

Therefore this story had to of occurred in the fall of 1937.

Sis and I were playing in the area of the smoke house and the smoke house. What were we doing I have no idea or than we were doing what kids do at that age. I remember seeing dad and Uncle Ethel walking down the hill beside the garden. I say hill but it is not really a hill but a gentle slope from the area of the old original barn that was on the farm when dad purchased the land.

Dad and Uncle Ethel were walking along slowly back toward the house and when they were half way down the slope I remember looking up and seeing a gun flying out over the garden. I could not believe my eyes, a flying shot gun. It landed about half way across the garden plot and come to a sudden stop on the ground.

Walking toward dad I remember him saying that the gun was no good and it wasn't carrying it into the house. I guess that explains why dad gave the gun a flying lesson. By the way this was the first time I had ever seen any thing get a flying lesson. What further compounds the situation was that I had never in my whole life seen dad upset over anything. Nothing!! Noda!! Zip point nothing!! By the way this was the last time that I ever saw dad upset to the point where he—gave the gun the flying lesson.

Being an enterprising young I beat feet into the garden and retrieved the gun. What happened to it I don't know. I know I carried it to the house. Where it went or how it went I have no idea. Never saw it again. Once again!! Nothing!! Noda!! Zip point nothing!! One day it was there and one day it wasn't.

The following Saturday dad came home from town. I didn't go so I have no idea where he went or what he had done. How ever when I noticed dad he was standing up on the hill about fifty yards from the old original barn and dad had a new gun. Well it was new to him because it had just gotten it some where. But the gun was not store bough ten brand new. It was indeed a used shot gun.

Dad shot the gun a couple of times toward the barn and his only response was, "it sure did kick a lot. Now how in the world can a shot gun kick? I really do not know but dad said his shoulder was hurting from just the two shots. Next time I saw the gun it had a pad on the end of the part that fits up to ones shoulder when firing the gun.

After, my father died the gun became mine. I don't have it now and I don't have any idea where it went to. I may have sold it or I may have given it to someone. I just can't remember!

I used dad's sixteen gauge shot gun a lot while growing up. And yes it did kick hard when the gun was fired. I put a larger pad on it and it still would leave your shoulder red when fired more than once or twice. It was a good old gun and shot true. That is all I can say for it.

Wish I had the gun back so I could pass it on to a family member; sorta keep it in the family so to speak.

FRIDAY NIGHT DATE

I am a strapping fifteen year old, in high school and playing freshman basketball. Being a young man I had looked at several young girls. They all looked nice but one stood out!!! She was quite a looker, as we called it in those days. She turned my head, was another expression used.

I did many things to gain her attention. Pushed her in the hallways. Pulled her hair, I wanted her to know that I thought she was the best-looking girl in the whole wide world. She had long shoulder length hair and beautiful deep brown eyes. I wanted to gain her attention and have her notice me.

I let some of her friends know that I liked her. That way she was bound to learn of my desire that she be my girl friend. It worked, now she knew and I think she sorta liked me too.

In Indiana during my era, there were not many sports the country schools offered. The big sport was basketball. I had tried out for the school team and was selected for the "B" team. That is where all of the freshman boys went except for some that had exceptional talents.

Wanting more than anything to be with this young lady I asked her to sit with me after the "B" basketball game was over. I did not have to worry too much about being sweaty or like that. I was a bench player. I sat on the bench mostly and cheered for our players with each goal scored. I was not sure she would be at the game. Her father was very strict. She was not sure that she would get to come.

After changing clothes I knew right where to look for her. I had made sure that I watched where she sat when she came in to the gym. I soon joined her after the "B" game was over. Was there an "A" game played?? I have no idea. My attention was elsewhere!!!

Postscript:

This gal became my wife the year we graduated from high school in 1950.

SUMMER SKY

As a kid did you ever lie on the ground and look at the sky? Did ever try to discern the different shapes of clouds? Did you ever find a cloud that looked like some person?

The wonders of a kid as they gaze skyward on a beautiful warm summer day. There is an airplane!! There is the—you name it and I have found it among the clouds.

To be young again and spend a lazy day staring upward at the clouds. It seems a million no make that gazillion years ago. As my sister and I would try to make different faces out of the clouds. There were so many and so many different shapes to run thought our memory.

So it is that the passage of time has taken away so many of the memories and all the different shapes and sizes that we once saw. Try as I might I can not recall all that we captured in out memories during those days.

A child can while away the time doing just about any thing. Lazily passing the hours away.

I know, I did it!! Those long days with out something to direct ones mind. The story of getting the truck out of the barn was but one of the moments that filled those days.

The library truck had come and gone. I had gotten my quota of five books and they were soon devoured. I mean reading every word. Going through them in just a matter of days. I always enjoyed reading and that was a good past time for me. Still I wish they would have let me have more books. Kids today do not know the joy of reading books. There is always the television. If it isn't the television then it is an epod, what ever that is.

Portable radios were not yet on the scene and so did not have any bearing on what we did.

Television is good but at the same time it is bad. There are so many programs to watch but at the same time. Most of the time a person does not know a day later what the story was about. Even to day I find it much more enjoyable to sit down with a good book. Right now I am reading a book that I had read several years ago. I find so much that I did not bet the first time through the book.

Ok so I read fast, some might call it speed reading. I am not really into that category but some times I do gloss over certain parts. Maybe the time I read the book I will find material that I did not get the first time around.

I wish more kids would like to read. I have traveled all over the world reading. I have learned much about so many different places. I truly do find a good book so enjoyable.

In school I did not read much as I listened in class and picked up most of the time that I did not have to study. It caught up with me in later years and I had to go back and learn what I should have gotten years ago.

I really started to learn what I had missed when I was twenty five years old. Pretty old for a high school student. But when I realized that I needed the information to be a better sailor. When my family and I went back into the navy in nineteen fifty eight I realized that I needed an education to help me advance in the navy.

I studied hard! I studied long! It took me three years to get to a high school level. I continued to study and took many math courses. I liked math in school but I did not retain much of the material taught.

I advanced through the rating I was working in, record time. I made advances as quickly as possible because it meant more money I would earn.

From those days of lazily watching the clouds until today I have learned so much yet I find the more I learn the less I know. Every time I work on a subject, I learn that there is so much more to learn!! The more I know the less I know!

Those lazy days of laying on ones back and simply watch clouds are gone. I long for those days. I think I would enjoy them even more now that I know what would lie ahead.

To every child in the world learn as much as you can in school. Enjoy each day as if it were to be your last.

PROUD TO BE AN AMERICAN

Where should this story start? Should it be back when very young and attended 4th of July parades? I was so proud to watch the parades with all the American flags flying. The weather was always warm so all of the little kids wore sun suits or other lightweight clothing.

Here comes the parade now the veterans with all their medals shining, leading. There were some five or six men all abreast, walking along. They did not march in time or step rather they seemed to sorta shuffle. There was proudness as they made their way along the street.

Horses with beautiful young women riding so eloquently in their western out fits. Men with their western garb, and their big cowboy hats.

Then came men carrying the American flags. Oh how I wanted to rush out and join them.

There was much more to the parade tractors decorated, cars decorated and hay wagons, too many to count.

After joining the navy in 1950 special emphases was given to our flag from my point of view. Each morning at 8:00 AM the flag was raised to the top of the flag pole. Every person within earshot came to attention and saluted the flag.

In the evening at sunset the whole base came to attention and saluted as the flag was lowered.

I partisapated in these events many times while serving four years at Naval Air Station Pensacola, Florida.

Just where in my naval career I became a flag waving American, I can't really pinpoint. There were the classes I was given to teach. Almost always there the subject came up.

I was proud of what I was doing, teaching classes for pilots and aircrew, for submarine anti-warfare. There was a new technique just received from the Canadians. Two sonabouys were dropped into the water a given distance from each other. A practice depth charge was dropped close by one of the sonabouys.

In the aircraft a high speed recorder was attached to the two receivers tuned to each sonabuoy. The explosion would cause the recording pen for the number one buoy to be deflected outward from the center of the recording paper. The sound would decay quickly with the pen moving back to the center of the paper.

Shortly afterward an echo could be heard and seen on the chart paper. The paper was moving at a given speed. The temperature of the water determines the speed of sound in the water. The temperature determined what ruler to use for the measurement from the beginning of the explosion to the echo traced on the paper.

A circle was drawn around the number one buoy on graph paper. Then the measurement from buoy number two was measured and them drawn. Where the two circles intersected is where the submarine is located.

Two different plots will give the direction and speed of the submarine. It was simple, and a good method to locate and attach a submarine.

This method is excellent for tracking a slow moving submarine. However the advent of the nuclear powered submarine and its high speed proved the tracking method know as "Julia" to be inadequate.

Shortly after the introduction of the nucular subs a new method was soon developed. This was code named "Jezebel". In fact even the names of the two systems were coded "Top Secret" They were never to be even mentioned out side the classroom.

The Jezebel tecquine required six different recording pens to analyze different sounds produced by the machinery on board the submarine.

Sodium pumps and other pieces of equipment used on nuceular submarines produced a unique signature for each class of enemy submarines.

How and where this information was gathered is still secret to this day.

This gives a brief overview of what I was teaching. In addition I was assigned the task of teaching underwater to the pilots and crew members.

I will add, at one time I started an underwater class when a Commander sitting in the back of the room informed me that a noncommissioned petty officer could not teach him anything.

Pretty poor attitude, for the senior member of the class to make such a statement. True I was a noncommissioned first class petty officer. But to make this statement in front of the whole class was inexcusable.

I called for a break and I headed straight to my departments senior officer. I was lucky he was in his office and I explained what had happened. He told me he would take care of the problem.

After the coffee bread I resumed teaching but the Commander was not there. The underwater sound lecture was two hours long. At the end of the first hour the commander came back to class but never said a word during the rest of the class.

Am I proud to be an American? YES I AM! Am I proud to live in the United States? YES I AM! Am I a flag waving American? YES I AM!

Do I stand at attention whenever our flag is presented? YES I DO!

If wearing a hat, it is removed and my right hand is placed over my heart.

I have seen many be disrespectful at many sporting events. Ever pay attention at a NASCAR the announcer asks every one to remove their hats. Most place their right hand over their heart.

Young people of today, that is most, do not have the pride for the greatest country in the world. Our country has the pleasure of being the best in the world.

I say; if you don't like the United States and what it stands for, GET OUT! Go to some of the third world countries and see what it is like to live there. Go live where there is no electricity. Go live where there is no running water in a house. Go live where there are no lines to carry off water and human waist.

Yes I am a flag waving American! Yes I love my country!

As the old country song goes!

GOD BLESS THE U.S.A.

SECTION II

LIFE

FAMILY MUSICIANS

Musical ability seems to be a part of my family. From my earliest memories, I remember Dad playing a guitar. There were many times that Dad would pull out the guitar and play old songs. I have a special memory of Dad playing his guitar, sitting on the couch as Mother was getting Sis and I, ready to go to town.

One of my first memories of music was at Mother's half sisters house. I believe it was at Aunt Clone's house. I know it was a true log cabin and it had three rooms. When you walked in the front door you were in the living room/sitting room/ bedroom. I do not remember much about the room, other than it had a wood burning heating stove.

Off this room to the left was a bedroom. That is where we kids were sent to sleep when we finally ran down. All I can remember of the room is that there was a bed and the room was semi-dark. I remember mother putting me to bed and pulling the covers over me to keep me warm.

To the right of the living room/sitting room/bedroom was the kitchen. There was a large wood-burning stove with an oven below. Above the cooking area was a warmer oven. To the right of the oven door was a tank, which was filled with water.

The men would gather in the kitchen to play their music, and the women would sit in the living room. Kids, well they were all about!! I do not recall playing outside. Perhaps we were too small to be allowed outside by ourselves. All of the memories I have of being there were after dark.

Many times, I recall standing in the kitchen beside Dad as he picked and played his guitar. Dad smoked and I can still see him in my mind to this day, stopping for a moment to take a drag from his cigarette then putting it in the ashtray on the floor. I would be standing just behind Dad's right shoulder.

There were several other men in the room with Dad, but I do not remember a name or face from those times. I wish I could!

Just after we moved to the farm Dad purchased a piano. It was placed into the already cramped space of the living room/ bedroom where Mother and Dad slept. Dad was soon picking out cords and began to play many different tunes. He was a natural musician.

Later Dad bought a mandolin, which has two strings for each tone. I do not recall when he purchased the fiddle but I remember him playing that also.

My sister, Barbara started taking lessons on an accordion. I do not remember how old she was, but I can tell you she was very young. I am almost sure that when she was older, the first accordion was traded in for a larger one, as she continued playing.

I learned to read music in grade school. I think I was in about the fifth or sixth grade. Mrs. Batchelor was the music teacher throughout all my years at the Smithville School.

Dad and Mother rented a trumpet to see if I would like to play it. They did not want to purchase one until making sure I would continue with it. I do not remember when the purchase was finally made. Perhaps they rented the trumpet with the option to buy. I think that is what they did.

When I joined the High School Band I started in the fourth chair, in my freshman year. I did not stay there long as Mrs. Batchelor moved me to second chair. I loved playing, but I only practiced at school. What could have happened if I had put some serious work into it, as I never pursued it after completing high school?

During my sophomore year I was once again advanced. I was moved to first chair this time. That made my day when the teacher moved me to first chair.

In my junior year I played many times in a duet, trio, or a quartet. The only person I can remember playing with is Bonnie Houston. We enjoyed playing together and became quite good.

I took band as often as they would let me, during study hour or any time I could get out of class. One year, I had band two periods in a row.

Two Country Bumpkins

My sister and husband had come to visit during Thanksgiving weekend, 2005. My wife had broken her leg earlier and was not able to go shopping, so plans were made for brother and sister to spend quality time together, shopping for the bargains early Friday morning since it had been years that they had gotten to be together. My wife and I had moved from American Canyon, California, the first of this year to Bloomington, Indiana, and my sister and family had lived in Hobe Sound, Florida for many years. This morning had to be the coldest morning Bloomington had had so far this year.

The night before we discussed what time we should get up to assure that we might be lucky in buying some of the bargains on my wife's list? Plans were made to start the round of stores by 6:00 a.m.

Going to bed that night, I thought to myself, 'that is too early', so I set the alarm for 6:00 a.m., thinking that would be early enough. So, what did I do but wake up at 5:30. I quickly got up and made a pot of coffee, which woke my Sis up. She asked if I was not early. "Yes" I replied and went on to get dressed so we could leave as soon as coffee was ready to drink.

The outside air temperature is hovering around 10 degrees. Brrrrr, it is, Cold!!!!!! What are we doing out on such a cold morning when we have been used to a much warmer climatic for so many years? We were going shopping for bargains for my wife and have quality time with my one and only sister. These was the only reasons we two were going out on such a cold morning, freezing our behinds off and have to deal with a herd of anxious shoppers.

Arriving at the first store it was not too crowded, so we dashed in and soon picked up two beautiful poinsettia plants. My wife had only requested one poinsettia, but knowing how well she likes them and the price was right, so we picked up two. Moving about the store we had to seek help in finding a microwave oven that was on sale too.

Having gone thorough the check out line we had only been in this store about twenty minutes. We are doing great, we thought. Dashing back to the truck we open the camper shell and sit our purchases inside the truck bed. (Remember now how cold it is this day!)

On to the next store we go! Pulling into the parking lot there was not an empty place to be found. Cars and trucks were parked everywhere. The only way to find a parking place was to follow someone leaving the store then wait until they loaded and backed out of their space. Luckily, we only had to wait about five minutes. What I did not realize is that if there are that many vehicles in the parking lot, then where are the owners, In the store, of course!

Once inside the store it was shoulder to shoulder with people. There were long lines at every check out counter.

Want a snow shovel? Stand in line to get one. On and on it went with most of the specials sold out. Toasters, sold out. Wrapping paper, gone.

We were in the store for more than one and a half hour. (Remember the poinsettias sitting in the cold in the back of the truck?)

We were dressed for the cold outside weather and now we are too hot for all the clothing we had on while inside the store. One step forward, then we wait! Another step forward and we wait some more. After thirty-five minutes we were within 10 feet of the checkout counter. Another fifteen minutes and we were finally checked out.

We are finally out the door and rush to the truck. It had been parked so long that the engine was now cold. We finally got home with our bargains, but quickly rushed them into the house as we were making a day trip down to Henderson, Kentucky area to see our son and his family. To our surprise when we returned home that night, the once lovely poinsettias were very much welted from frostbite. So my idea of buying two was not such a good idea after all.

Much teasing has come from the family that you do not send a Floridian and a Californian to buy poinsettias on one of Indiana's coldest mornings, especially if they are going to leave them in the back of a truck bed for several hours. But all was not in vain, as fond memories were made by brother and sister that morning. It was almost like being young again.

FRED'S THOUGHTS AND DESIRES

I want to take this time to state some of my thoughts and desires. In some writings such as the "If, 55 Acres" story, I put on paper some of my basic desires. I want to use this now to set forth, somewhat better, my views and thoughts.

Is it wrong to want to settle in a comfortable retirement home? I think not. Does it go against what one knows? Again I think not.

What I envision is a small acreage, maybe five to 100 acres of land but would much prefer twenty some acres. There must be room enough that you will not see houses in any direction. I do not want to hear neighbors driving in their driveway. I do not want to hear neighbors arguing or quarreling. I do not want to look up and see a neighbor looking at me. Is this so wrong?

I want to be able to walk in my backyard and know that I am alone. I want to be able to walk about a piece of land and not have to worry about someone robbing me. I want to watch the natural growth of plants, shrubs, and flowers. I want to watch small animal's scurry about doing what it is they do. I want to watch birds as they go about their daily existence, building nests, feeding their young and protecting them.

I want to see ducks and geese as they fly high overhead in their formations, searching out a place to feed or roost for the night. I want to watch squirrels as they seek trees that have an abundance of nuts they like to feed upon. I want to sit and watch as they scamper through the upper most limbs in search of food.

I want to watch the trees bud and new leaves began to take shape. I want to see them grow to full maturity and sway in a gentle breeze. I want to watch the tree branches sway as a storm moves them. I want to watch the leaves turn colors in the fall after a frost has set in. I want to watch them fall as winter approaches. I want to watch as the wind blows then into hedgerows or piles in a quiet corner.

I want to see the dogwood trees in early spring displaying their blooms with bursts of color. I want to see the dogwoods, the maples, the oaks, and all the others as they come to life after an early April rain.

I want to see thunderstorms roll in from the west. Skies turning dark with the low dense clouds filled with moisture. Hear the rolling thunder as it booms in the distance. See the dazzling displays of lighting, as it flashes across the sky.

I do not need concrete under my feet, nor do I need parking lots so huge that you cannot find your car, when you come out of a store. I do not like to go shopping and have to elbow your way through the people to get what you want. I do not need people and their rudeness. I want to walk and not be afraid that you will be robbed going to your car. Much less sit in your home and worry that you must keep everything locked in fear.

People are in such a hurry any more that they are demanding wherever they are, on highways, in town or small community. People are not courteous. Everyone seems to be for self and give no thought as to how they respond to anyone else.

All I would like to have is a place to call my own, small piece of land, where I can walk and watch nature go about her business.

I want to be able to sit in the evenings and watch the sun go down. I would like to sit on a porch and see the rain falling. I would like to be able to put on a raincoat and go strolling in a spring rain shower.

I want to be able to sit inside and see snow on the ground. I want to see snowdrifts. I want to see my breath in the air as I exhale when out on a cold winter day. I want to have to put on a heavy coat to protect against the cold winter wind. I want to have to hurry from the car to the house on a cold winter evening.

I want to rise early and watch the sun come up over the horizon. Watch the sky change colors as the night passes to early morning light. I want to hear the stillness and the oneness of the beginning of another day.

I want to walk beside a stream of water. I want to see the creatures that live there. I want to watch as they meander along. I want to see the moss growing on a boulder or a small rock. I want to see small fish as they dart back and forth searching for food. I want to follow the stream and know it's every turn, where the water rushes and pushes against some lodged tree limbs or leaves which diverts its flow.

I want to sit beside the stream and daydream. I want to feel the warmness of the sun as it peeks through the treetops. I want to feel the serenity of not having to be at work or at any particular place any given time.

I want to take walks, just to see what is over the next hill. I want to view a particular place from many different angles, approaching from many directions until I know what each view offers. I want to stroll down a country lane and not have to hurry.

I want to be there, just to be there.

Last Coon Hunt with Dad

I can't remember what year it was but Dad asked if I would like to go on a coon hunt with him. Dad did not have coon hounds, not one. We only had a little dog that originally started out with the name of Fuzzy. That's right Fuzzy.

He was orphaned at about four weeks old. His mother a pure breed Husky was killed leaving a family of four little puppies that would surely die if not adopted and bottle fed until big enough to eat regular food.

The neighbor across the street from us brought the little puppy to our home for some love and care. Soon he was eating as good as an eight week old pup.

Name? Why he was a little fuzzy ball of fur when he came to live with us. That's how he came to be called Fuzzy. I loved that little dog. Everywhere I went Fuzzy went as well. I tucked him into a jacket pocket or carried him like a little baby. He did not like to lie on his back, so he set on my arm or my hand.

Whenever I would leave the house, that dog was always at my heals. I could not sneak away from him.

So it was, that we had this housedog that was not a house dog. Mother did not want him in the house. So, I would sneak him in and go to my room. After a while mother gave up and let him have the run of the house.

This is the only dog that dad had now. After I had left home Fuzzy stayed and became a part of Mother and Dad's lives.

This is the dog that dad and I took out to go coon hunting. Fuzzy loved to chase anything that would run away from him. We were in for an interesting night of hunting.

We crossed the back fence of our property and turned north toward the backside of what is now the Starlight drive-in theater on old Hwy 37. Fuzzy was running around sniffing at a whole lot of nothing. He didn't know how to smell out a trail. He was not one bit of a hound. If there is such a thing as a sight hound, this he was.

We walked and he sniffed. He sniffed and we walked. Running every which direction but always staying close to dad and me.

This went on for over an hour until Dad said that it was time to head back home.

Narry a coon had been treed, narry a rabbit was disturbed, nor was any other animal found. Fuzzy could not even track a biscuit, much less a coon.

But Dad and I had a good time being with each other. We enjoyed the time of just being together.

I had the best dad that a boy could ever have.

LIFE IS SO SHORT

There are those that don't know it
Time moves so swiftly
Stop to smell the roses
Take the time to look about

Look at a tree and admire its beauty
Listen to the birds as they sing
Spend a moment to listen to nature
Creatures as they scurry about

Can you spare the time?
To care about someone else?
Say a word of kindness
Ask about their life

Listen and not worry about yours
Give them the attention you want
It will return a thousand fold
With Blessings untold.

Be thankful for each morning
Thankful that your eyes open
Ears that can hear
And voice to share with others

Stop and listen to your heartbeat
Look at the beauties that abound
As the day begins to unwind.
Be thankful that you can

LITTLE GIRL & HER GO-KART RIDE

A seven-year-old girl always wanted to do what her older brother and sister were doing. Sometime about 1963 her family had been vacationing with relatives in Indiana. While there the father bought a go-kart from one of the relatives.

It was nice as go-karts go. It was painted red and had been raced by a high school classmate of the parents of the little girl. The engine was damaged but it was a good buy.

This little girl was a bubbly enthusiastic person. She was always right in the middle of whatever was going on. She was the perfect addition to a family.

One day the father had removed the old engine from the go-kart. He temporarily installed a four-cycle engine so the children would be able to drive the go-kart. The engine was hooked up direct drive. In other words, the kart had to be pushed to get the engine started.

The brother and older sister had taken turns riding the go-kart around a small track that the father had made in the backyard. It was a dirt track but one where the kids could go fast enough to make the back end slide out if they wanted to.

Finally the father decided that they had ridden enough and was planning to take the go-kart back to the house. They lived in the country and there was an extended driveway in front of their house. The kart was stopped on the dead-end of the driveway. The driveway sloped for about a hundred yards down to the county road.

This little girl was complaining that she had not ridden the go-kart yet. She was making such a fuss that the father decided to let her ride the kart down the slope and into the garage. Actually it was not a garage, but a carport. It had a concrete surface and a brick outer wall about three feet high. On the back end of the carport was an opening into the backyard.

The little girl is seated on the go-kart. She is instructed that the right foot pedal make it go faster or slower and the left foot pedal is the brake. Very simple to remember!

She had seen the procedure for starting the engine. Father would pick up the back end of the kart. Run for two or three steps, sit the rear wheels on the ground, and push on the back of the seat until the engine started. He explains that there is no worry. He will be right there all the time.

She is to turn into the carport driveway and stop the kart. She nods her head as the instructions are given. Yes, she understands how to operate the gas pedal! Yes, she knows how to use the brake!

Picking up the rear of the kart the father starts to run. After two steps he sits the rear wheels on the ground. The engine starts. Father is right there with his hand on the rear of the seat. He is running to stay with the kart. Pretty soon he is running as fast as he can. They are just about to the carport drive. It is all he can do to keep up. The kart picks up more speed. Now it is all the father can do to keep one hand on the kart.

The driveway is coming up fast. He begins yelling "Put on the brakes, push on the brake pedal." The little girl now has doubts about which pedal to push. She pushes on the right pedal even more. The kart goes even faster!!

They are almost at the driveway. The little girl turns the steering wheel suddenly and swiftly and enters the carport driveway. Now the father cannot keep up with the kart. He is two steps behind and running for all he is worth, no, three steps behind, now four!!

The kart and little girl are now in the carport. OH NO, she is not slowing down!!!!! There is the wall on the back end of the carport. She is going to crash into the wall!!

Quicker than the blink of an eye the kart and little girl are through the narrow opening and out into the back yard safely. The opening is only four inches wider than the kart. (The father later measured the opening and the width of the kart.)

The little girl and her kart went through that opening at about fifteen MPH, then down a step and into the back yard. I would never have guessed that going that fast she could ever have judged it sooooo RIGHT!!!!

The father was relieved when the kart came to a halt in the back yard. The little girl was terror-stricken and the tears begin to flow! With the father's comforting arms around her, he began to explain to her the mix up with the pedals caused her to go too fast for father to keep up.

She did not get to ride the go-kart for sometime after that. In fact she never asked.

Postscript

This little girl, my youngest daughter Suzi, grew up and was one of the most ardent fans of her brother Steve, during his racing career. She was there every time the car went to the track. She and her husband helped make up the pit crew.

She drove the racecar in several races. Later a second racecar was built and she and others in the pit crew took turns driving the car. Her husband drove the regular racecar as well. He would have made a fine racecar driver in his own right. Too bad, that racing ended for the family before he had a chance to prove himself.

Dearest "Sis"

I was at the computer when your email came. It was so wonderful to read your words. Someone else feels as I do. I think it has something to do with how we were raised.

We did a lot of exploring not only on our farm but also Mr. Meadow's fields and valleys. The old seemingly abandoned farm where our twin cousins Peggy and Patsy lived, we were all over that farm. Hunting mushrooms and picking wild flowers, which were in abundant supply in the springtime.

I remember we were with Dad's sister, Mary and her kids one time. She was looking for Ginseng plants. The roots were worth a lot of money. She and her husband made extra money that way.

Do you remember that Uncle Edgar and his family lived in the old farmhouse as well as the log cabin up close to where the gravel road forked? Do you ever remember being in that log cabin? It was just one large room. There was a rope strung across where they hung sheets and blankets to divide the room into sleeping quarters. Do you remember any of this?

It must have been spring because cousin Loran took me to see a tiny mushroom he had found. He did not pick it, but said he wanted to see if it would grow larger.

Now back to your letter. Yes I agree that there should be a stream of water going through the property such as depicted in my ('If 55 Acres' story). Enough woods where one could walk and not worry about seeing anyone else.

The only area that is left in Indiana where country wilderness is cheap enough that I could afford to buy is around Crane. That is where the 55 acres is located that I was writing about.

Thank you for responding so quickly. I am writing a story about the musical talent in our family. I will send it for you to review. Please add as much as you would like to it.

I am enjoying writing about my early years. Maybe I am reverting back to my childhood. Who knows! You are a good writer too, so I hope to read some of your stories. I know you can add to mine as well. That would make it interesting for our children in later years.

Your Loving Brother,
Frederick

SCHOOL BUS

My first day going to school I had to ride the school bus. I don't remember the first years. I know that aunt Margaret was with me as I boarded the bus. Where do I sit? What do I say? How do I act? I don't have the vaguest idea of what I did.

I had no idea as I had never been through an exercise like it before. It was not unpleasant. I soon made friends and soon was sharing a seat with them.

Upon reaching the school the bus pulled up directly in front of the door. Kids of all ages were streaming out of a full bus load.

Into the front door there people directing first timers to their class room. My room happened to be on the second floor and the first door on the right.

I remember being assigned a seat. I remember sitting there like a bump on a log. Lunch pail in hand. Looking first to the left and them to the right.

After a while I started enjoying going to school. It was easy and it was fun to learn.

I had a wonderful teacher. Strange I can not remember her name. I think it was Mrs. Humphrey but I am not sure.

Soon the day was over and we were directed to go directly to the school bus we had arrived on.

I really don't remember the bus drivers during the early years.

Mr. Kinser purchased a bus and picked up kids from Harrodsburg, up highway 37 (what is known now as old 37) and on to the school.

Mr. Kinser was a very good driver. He was fast but never was cause for alarm. The only strange thing about him and it is not really strange, he only had one eye. How or when he lost the eye was not known. He could judge better than most people with two eyes.

He drove his bus to basketball games, to the skating rink and many other events. I do know he drove to the Fall Festival at Ellettsville each year. I remember the first year I went to the festival as a member of our high school band.

I played a trumpet and really enjoyed the experience all four years of high school.

Back to Mr. Kinser, we kids were always complaining about the bus being cold. Really, really cold! I believe this was during my freshman year.

What happened next is that we boarded the bus one early one morning and there was a strange two inch pipe running along one side of the aisle. It was hot, NO I MEAN REALLY HOT! We were told to not put our shoes on the pipe. To never let our skin touch the pipe.

Now what does any energetic kid do? If told to not touch the wet paint out come a figure into the paint. Not to put our shoe on the pipe, surely we must set our shoe on the pipe to test it out.

Many of us had a burnt path across the ball of the shoe. The smell was not pleasant as well. Still each child on the bus had to test putting a shoe on the hot pipe.

Sugar Cured Meat

Some meat was canned and so were 'cracklings'. When a hog is butchered for winter meat, all of the fat is saved and cut into cubes about an inch square. A large kettle is placed upon three support stones outside and a fire is built beneath it. The fat cubes are placed in the kettle. As the lard is released from the cubes it becomes almost a clear liquid. When all of the lard is 'rendered' the remainder of the fat will turn a golden brown. Cracklings are then removed with a large sieve. Mother canned many two-quart jars of cracklings. They became a tasty treat to eat as soon as they cooled from being dipped from the hot fat.

Just before placing the lid on the canning jars, it was filled almost to the top with the hot liquid lard. This was a convenient way to store both lard and the cracklings. When mother made corn bread she added cracklings to it. The remaining liquid lard was dipped into five-gallon metal cans where it cooled and a lid was placed on top to keep the lard clean. The lard was used as needed for cooking until next autumn's hog butchering and lard rendering time.

My father-in-law did an extra step to help purify the liquid lard. His wife would peel several pounds of small potatoes. These were placed in the boiling lard where they were cooked to a golden brown. These were delicious and never made it to the dinner table as too many standing by were eager to eat them as they were cool enough to eat.

Rendering lard is a time consuming process. The fire must be maintained at a proper temperature. If the fire is too hot the lard will have a burned taste. Normally two or more hogs were butchered at a time. Rendering was started early in the morning and was never finished until late in the day.

There was also sausage to be ground up. When the main parts of the hog were being cut and trimmed, any trimmings that had some lean meat along with the fat were placed in a special pan. This is what was used for sausage. Too much fat was removed and placed in the pan for rendering

We had a hand turned sausage grinder. Sitting there for hours one would stuff meat trimmings into the top of the grinder, and turn the handle to cause it to grind up as it came out the other end. It was not a clean job, because as the meat adjusted to room temperature it becomes very greasy and difficult to handle. Soon hands would be dripping with grease. This helped soothe chapped hands, which was common during winter months.

Hogs were most always butchered late in the fall. Many times the temperature fell below freezing during the nights. After the hogs were cleaned and cut into halves they were hung overnight to firm up the meat before cutting them into different parts. Hams, shoulders, pork chops and sides of bacon needed more work to preserve them for the winter meat.

My father always sugar cured all of the cuts of meat. A mixture of sugar, black pepper, red pepper and salt were mixed in a large pan. White muslin cloth was measured out large enough to wrap the piece of meat several times. Next, newspaper or white wrapping paper was laid on the muslin cloth. The paper must completely encase the cut of meat. This is then covered with a liberal sprinkling of the salt mixture. Then the cut of meat is laid on paper with the skin side down on the salt mixture. A liberal amount of the salt mixture is rubbed into every nook and cranny of the meat.

The paper is carefully folded around the meat, followed by the muslin cloth. Pins were used to hold the cloth tightly in place. A strong string cradle was tied about the bundle so the cut of meat could be hung up in the same position, as it was when on the animal. If the meat is hung upside down or crossways the fluids in the meat will not drain and cause it to spoil.

After the hams, shoulders, bacon slabs were ready to hang; it is now time to smoke them. If the meat is not smoked it is hung in a cool place until needed.

Many times I've watched mother take a ham down, cut off several slices of meat, wrap it back up and hang the ham from the rafter in the smokehouse.

If one was fortunate enough to have a walk in freezer it was great. Our freezer was the smokehouse. Another place that was quite cold in the winter was the small room where I slept. Meat was also hung there against the outer wall.

Yes, it was a very cold room. If snow fell with a north wind blowing I woke up many mornings with snow on the floor and across the bed.

THE "IF" 55 ACRES STORY!

Some folks would think lots of acreage would mean lots of upkeep for them. Nothing could be farther from the truth. Most of the land would not need any work done. Leave it as nature directs.

The house could be located in a small clearing and the only yard work would be to keep whatever area one desired, mowed. Around the outside of the house could be much the way my brother in law, Dan has his yard with shrubbery. Actually, he has too much to maintain but must do so to keep it looking neat in the neighborhood.

What I envision would be a small area around the house and workshop. Two or three flower beds if there is enough light available. I would like some shrubs, plants, or flowers along the driveway. This could be difficult to accomplish if there are deer in the area. The same would be true of a garden plot.

Two outside dogs, well cared for and with houses for each, would be nice. The dogs could serve several purposes, such as companionship, when out side working or exploring the property. They could also keep deer and other animals away from the garden and house.

I would like salt blocks for the deer in an area away from the house, and feeders set up for birds and squirrels. Birdhouses of all sorts located around the area. Big ones as well as little ones, some painted, some not.

If they were no quail in the area I would purchase several pairs of birds and reintroduce them to the area. I would need many brush piles to give the birds and small animals shelter. A cat would be needed to keep small rodents away from the house area.

Dependent upon where a stream of water is located on the property, a dirt road to the stream would be nice. Simply driving along a given path several times will make a road. Dirt roads require no maintenance. The up-keep would be filling in potholes to prevent getting stuck during wet weather.

What I envision would be a clearing at or near the stream. Picnic lunches would be nice there. The musical sound of water traversing the rocks is always pleasant. Dependent upon the size of the stream, a small dam constructed of rock and debris could easily be made, forming a wadding pool in the stream. Not too big, just enough so you could take your shoes off and dip your feet into the cool clear water.

When our children and grandchildren or folks come to visit we could take them for a picnic. There would be a need for a couple of picnic tables left in the clearing to be used as needed for such occasions.

The house must have a large front porch with a swing. The porch would need to be screened to keep out bugs and mosquitoes. The house should be small and easily maintained. It should have a large area, which would include the family room, kitchen and dining area all in one.

The house must have good insulation. Exterior walls should be of stone or brick and roof of long lasting material. Everything should be low maintenance.

Let me stop for a moment and try to put into words what it is like to walk into a wooded area. A morning stroll into the woods, with no desire to reach a given point at any time, can be so uplifting.

Look at the trees with their hues of deep green! There are new leaves with lighter shades of green. Sunshine is reaching through; to brighten the leaf covered soil.

Stop! Be still!! Listen to the birds as they sing their early morning songs. Mates are calling to each other, or just sitting in the trees. A blue jay calls its distinctive song.

Move gently through the low hanging branches of an oak. Perhaps skirt around a dense bunch of young trees vying to see who can be the quickest reaching upward to the sky.

Wild grapevines clinging to a tall hickory tree are reaching out to grasp any branch it can.

Look at the spring flowers as they spread their petals, their blooms are bursting open to expose delicate centers. Lambs tongue, May-apples with their twin blossoms, oh there is so much to admire!

Hickory, oak, maples, sassafras each have their own growth pattern and with distinctive shape. All are fully filled out in their finest and each leaf turned to gather sunlight.

It is wonderful to stand quietly in a wooded area, teeming with life of all sorts of nature. Wipe away the leaves from the base of a tree and watch small creatures scurrying to seek a safe haven.

One can only experience what I have tried to describe, by going through the experience too. Words do not do justice in describing the scene.

In the busy world we find ourselves in today, there is no time to experience what I knew as a young boy. There is little or no time for viewing a sunset, or rain falling softly through the canopies of the trees.

Walk in a soft falling rain and hear raindrops as they fall on the leaves, creating the most beautiful music. One can hear the soft pattering as each drop adds to the chorus.

In the spring, don a hat, raincoat and rubber boots to keep the feet and clothes dry. No worries about where each foot is placed. Walk in puddles of water! Feel the raindrops on your face and enjoy the solitude and of being one of God's creatures as you take this walk.

May I always have the desire to seek out the beauty of nature and to smell the earth as it gives off dank and pungent odors. The joy of walking through an open meadow, with gentle breezes, swaying plants, and flowers is so dazzling. Then gaze toward distant hills. A picture any artist could portray on canvas!

Blackberries are relished by humans and animals alike. Possums, skunks, weasels and cows, seek the tender morsels. Pies and cobblers are made for the enjoyment of young and old.

Soil is tilled and gardens are planted. Fresh vine ripe tomatoes are eagerly awaited. Green beans, corn, beets and more are soon to arrive. Each will add distinctive tastes to the palate.

The fall season brings color to the leaves with wonderful hues of reds, yellows and oranges. The trees are preparing to shed those once green leaves.

Crisp mornings, with frost evident, helping the change from summer to winter for plant life. Squirrels and birds are busily storing nuts from the oak and hickory trees. Animals and humans alike store black walnuts.

Walk in the winter snow! See the wondrous view of trees with snow piled on the branches. Gaze across meadows with skiffs of snow weighing heavily on the now brown summer plants but hardly discernable under their coats of white.

Watch the snowflakes as they fall! Their graceful, spiraling descent produces majestic mantles of white and accumulates on any surface wide enough to support them. Icicles are hanging from eves with their rippled surface, clear and are cold to the touch.

Each day is a new beginning as we travel through life! Now that I am older I want to live the life of gentle pleasures. To be able to see, to feel, and to know once again, nature as it is, when left undisturbed.

Trees, great and powerful, with much splendor, will one-day fall. To will be replaced by one much younger, seeking out the essence of life.

So it is with each of us, the day will come when it is our turn. To be replaced by a younger person. Taking their steps through life until it is time for them to go, then replaced once again.

Words cannot describe what is in my heart! Am I, wanting to seek out what once was? Do I seek something unattainable? I think not. It is the simple pleasures sought as life winds down toward the end, plus the privilege of reminiscing what was the past.

Bowel of Cherries

Forest Gump said "Life is like a box of chocolates, when you take out a piece of candy you never know what you will get."

For me life is like a bowel of cherries. Smile while reaching into the bowel; it is unlikely you will get a lemon. Smile and the world will be better for it. But, if you get a lemon make lemonade and then smile.

Author unknown
By request of the author

CHARLESTON, SOUTH CAROLINA

In nineteen sixty six while stationed at Naval Air Station Memphis I had taught closed circuit television in the advanced Tradevman school. I have written elsewhere about my tour there. I worked with a senior chief petty officer who was friends with the assignment desk senior chief petty officer. I talked my senior chief into helping me get my specialty field classification changed to include CCTV.

The navy was installing nine CCTV training schools and one of them was located at Charleston, South Carolina. I wanted to get out of Memphis something bad. I had had enough of the eight hours teaching each day. When you have a senior chief as your teaching partner you seldom had any help because they were always off doing what ever it is that they do when they do not want to teach. I was an E 6 and the senior chief was an E 8, you did not tell them much of anything.

A couple of weeks later I was informed that I had transfer orders, to report to the personnel office to review them and find out where I was going to be transferred. Charleston, South Carolina it was, I would be leaving in about a month. I rushed home to tell my wife and family about our up coming move.

GOLD PANNING

What can be more exciting than to find GOLD in a pan of gravel? I know of nothing that can and will make the spirits soar. I remember the first few specks of gold in the bottom of the pan. But that is getting way ahead of where the story begins.

There is a creek high in the Serra Mountains named Bull Creek that I started camping along side of back in the late nineteen sixties. Two fellows I worked with at the NAS Lemoore Naval Air Station. Which is located in the middle of California, out in the desert I was told before arriving at the base? Yes it is arid land, little or no surface water except with is channeled in from the mountains. It was far more civilized than what I had imagined.

Back to the two fellow workers at the station, they were fascinated by the stories of old gold mines. They spent five days exploring the area, looking for what ever they could find at the old abandoned mines. Arriving back at work the following Monday we were soon comparing areas where they had found mines.

The area they were searching was almost a wilderness area. For anyone with knowledge of the gold mining area the gold where the gold came to the surface followed a more or less path where highway forty-nine is presently located.

A small gold mining town named Coulterville sits at a crossroads. Traveling southward right in the middle of the town a left turn is made. It is twenty two miles to the site which is where my two work companions camped.

First the road is blacktop, then it turns to gravel then the last mile is a dirt road. When we first started going to the area there is a small side stream that must be forded to continue higher in the mountains. There was a small clearing where the two streams of water joined. At that time it was necessary to have a fire permit to build a fire. There was a ranger station on the way in and each time we would stop and get our fire permit.

It was a lovely area; pristine in fact, brush grew along side the road making it a single lane. There were no homes in the area as it is in the nation forest. Once there had been people that built small buildings for homes during the early nineteen thirties. Actually they were located on mining claims during those hard days of the depression.

On my first trip there I traveled with the two working companions. We took my truck and camper with a trailer to haul three motorcycles. On this first trip we did not have gold pans. Didn't even know what a gold pan looked like.

We traveled in all directions looks for the gold mines that had been found earlier on their trip. We were always trying to locate gold mines that no one had picked apart.

It was a delightful week and the three of us traveled many miles on the dirt roads. Soon our time was gone and we had to return back to the base for the following week work schedule.

Many trips were taken that summer and the following one. On one such trip we located a long sluice chute that showed there had been a tremendous effort to remove gold from the nearby Bull Creek. The sluice chute was about a hundred fifty feet long. The bottom of the sluice was five feet off the ground, with four foot sides to contain the water and gravel the was directed in to it.

We could find no evidence of how the water was redirected into the sluice but it surely was. Also there was no evidence of where the gravel exited the chute.

It was most exciting to try to determine how it all taken place. A lot of work had been done to build a large sluice at this site. It was located in a small meadow which ran about two hundred yards along side the creek.

I received transfer orders to Naval Base Mare Island and my family and I moved in the summer of nineteen seventy two to the near by town of Vallejo. I talked with some members at the division I was assigned to and soon a camping trip was being organized. My future son-in-law was a part of the group (did not know at that time that he would become a part of the family.

Dan had a motorcycle at the time and did not have a secure place to keep the bike and tools. I offered a small spot in my garage for him to park the bike and tools.

More than half of the people assigned to our division wanted to make the trip as well. I organized the efforts for food, water, gas and much more as we prepared to camp out for the week end. I had two small motorcycles and several opted to take their cycles as well. We had a large group and with the motorcycles my small trailer was full.

It was a great weekend and everyone took turns riding the motorcycles. There was a large meadow some three miles up the dirt road and we all as a group traveled to the meadow to allow everyone to explore the many dirt roads that lead into the meadow.

Returning home Sunday afternoon it took a long time to get every thing unpacked and stored away. Dan hung around after everyone else had left and we started to talk about another trip to the same area. Soon another trip was planned but this time we decided that we would buy gold pans and try our hand at trying to find some gold.

Keep in mind that he or I had any idea about how to pan for gold. I bought a booklet on how to claim a portion of land "a mining claim" and how to go about registering the claim. There were no details on how to pan or where to even start looking for gold. All we knew was that gold was much heavier than all the various rocks and sand.

Therefore it would drop to the bottom of a creek or in our instance to the bottom of a gold pan with movement or the passing of water causing the sand to shift therefore the gold would settle quickly to solid rock or the bottom of the gold pan.

We bought gold pans and were ecstatic about getting back up to the gold country to try our luck at panning. Little did we know that we would make many trips before we found any specks of gold.

We took my truck and camper which required that we pull a trailer with the motorcycles in it. We took Dan's small truck and slept in the back of it. We would pan for a while then ride motorcycles for a while. Still we had only found a few little specks of gold to show for all our efforts.

We were looking in all the wrong places; we would take a shovel of gravel from the top of the gravel bank. We went up stream, we went down stream, and we stopped and rode motorcycles until it was time to go home.

On one such trip we were panning near our camp site when an older man happened by. He asked if we had found any gold. Our prompt reply caused him to laugh and he told us we were looking in the wrong places as well as we really didn't know how to work the pan either. He gave us friendly advice on where to look and how to swirl the pan to help separate the gravel and sand quickly as possible.

We had worked our butts off with out finding hardly a few specks of gold. One of the places he advice us to work was along side the creek bed. Into the grass and weeds that grew along side the little creek of water. Soon we were doing just that and started to find a few small specks of gold. Advice was given to take the grass and weeds and let them dry and burn them. Pan the ashes for the flour gold that had become imbedded in them. We did find some small, very small specks of gold but it really wasn't worth the effort.

On another one of our trips to the same area we found that a group of men were camped in the spot that we usually occupied. We drove further down the meadow and camped under a large oak tree. A perfect for a family to camp. The ground was fairly level and there was not vegetation that might catch fire. We had gathered many fairly large rocks and formed a fire pit.

Later that evening I walked back to the area where the other group was camped and they told me that they were on a trial run to test their equipment before they would go to Grass Valley and treck several miles back into rather remote territory. I was interested in seeing how more professional gold panners would go about separating the gold from the creek bed.

I could hardly wait until the next morning as that was when they were going to try out their equipment.

Arising as to what I thought was early I could hear the gas engine driving their retrieval equipment already. They had a sluice box about six feet long with water running through it. The gas engine was driving a rather large suction pump. On the suction end was attached a four inch plastic flexible hose. Fairly stiff enough to cause the person holding the pipe to have to work fairly hard at keeping the hose directed to the area they wanted to vacuum the sand and gravel.

Even more interesting was the fact that the person holding the end of the long vacuum hose was dressed in a wet suit. I knew what a wet suit was as I had seen many people surfing along the coast near the cliff house restaurant sitting on the bluff of the Pacific Ocean southeast of San Francisco. The water was cold there just as it was running in the little stream called Bull Creek.

The water was rushing very fast through the sluice box, which was the discharge side of the pump. I stood in fascination and watched the men operate the rig for about forty five minutes. They shut down the pump and proceeded to inspect the inside of the sluice box. To my surprise there was indoor/outdoor carpet running the complete length of the box.

All of the surface gravel and sand was quickly brushed way. Peering intentionally at the matting they quickly picked out some larger pieces of gold and placed them into a small glass jar, about two inches in diameter. It was about half full of gold and make my eyes bug at how much they had collected. When I inquired if all of it had come from this spot on the creek they all smiled and said no most of it had come on another trip they had made the weekend before.

The carpet was quickly rolled up and tied and tucked away in their camper, with comment that it would be cleaned after the were home, Much to our disappointment they informed Dan and I that this creek must have been worked before by a very good group. They believed that what they were finding had been deposited recently during a heavy rain fall a couple of weeks before.

Dan and I gave up on the main run of Bull Creek but did manage to make several "finds" on the little creek that ran across the road and into Bull Creek. We worked the banks mainly and that is where I found the largest piece of gold that I collected during all of my trips to the gold country.

When Dan and I were at work the following week we were racking our brains of where we could locate a gasoline driven suction pump. It was a concern that the sand and gravel would be pulled through the pumping vanes. Just any old ordinary suction pump would be destroyed quickly with all of the sand much less the larger pieces of gravel.

We though that we might make a find at the salvage yard on the base. Arriving at the site we started searching for a gas powered suction pump. We finally found two that we though might be able to handle the sand and gravel.

That evening we tried out one of the pumps in my back yard. It didn't have as much suction as we had hoped but really it was all we could afford at the time. It did pump water through a two inch hose; it did put out a goodly supply of water. We planned a trip for the following week end. But we were going to try another area that would not have as much traffic as the Bull Creek area. It was getting quite popular and always had people going up and down the dirt road.

Dan had built two sluice boxes which were about eight feet long. The bottom was about twenty inches wide with eight inch sides. In side the box there were one and half inches high and wide. They were attached every six inches the whole length of the box. The bottom and sides were cut out of three quarter inch plywood. They were heavy to carry but we thought it would stand up better to the rigors of what we were going to do.

As I said we went to another area that was in the gold region but less traveled. We set up camp after arriving rather late but then we decided to explore the roads with our motorcycles. I owned two Honda Trail nineties, a good bike to explore with as it handled good on or off road.

Dan started off in the lead and it was all I could do to keep up with him. Sometimes I didn't keep up and Dan would have to stop and wait for me to catch. We rode like this for what seemed like hours but in it was just over an hour. Finally we called it a night and slept in the back of his pickup truck. If you have never slept on the hard metal bed of a pickup truck I would you to never do it.

Early the next morning we rushed through a brief breakfast and set up our equipment. We didn't use the sluice box but directed the discharge water on the sloping exposed bed rock sloping into the creek. One of the problems we had was that rocks larger than the intake would block the pickup. Later we found that the smaller rocks and gravel were destroying the impeller on the pump. After about two hours of fighting this setup we decided that this was not the way to hunt for gold.

Later on another trip to Bull Creek I was up the small stream that crossed the road about a hundred yards or so. Sitting on the bank I had been working the grass and weeds that grew along the creek. I would pull clumps of the grass and weeds and clean then into my gold pan. I had worked for over and hour and finally had the pan full of sand and some gravel. I started working the pan around and around dipping it into the water with each circle of the pan that helped was the top layer of larger rocks out and back into the creek. Finally I had the mixture down to just a little white sand and a lot of black sand. Working slowly now, I moved the layer of white sand completely out of the pan. The white sand it much lighter than black sand and of course any gold that might be at the bottom of the pan.

Suddenly I saw a speck of gold appear, I kept the water moving slowly around the pan and the speck got bigger. I moved more sand and the gold piece kept getting larger and larger. When it was completely uncovered it was a quarter of an inch long and about an eighth of an inch wide. I was beside myself. I had never found more than eighth inch long piece of gold in my whole life.

Just about that time I heard someone calling that supper was ready. I so happy at my find and started toward the campsite. I was a pretty sight, no shirt on, knee rubber boots and I was rushing as quickly as possible to show everyone what I had in my gold pan. Much to my surprise there was not much interest in the gold; they were all Hungary and ready to eat. Sure was a let down but I still had my lump of gold.

This story would not be complete with out telling about the "Midnight Panning for Gold story". On this trip to the gold country my son Steve and his two boys Steve Jr. and Jeremy as well as two boys who lived across the street Bunky and Bugger. Not their real names but that what their parents called them. I have forgotten their given names.

We set up camp in the meadow close to the bank of Bull Creek. The boys all grabbed their fishing poles and were fishing for trout. The stream is stocked every two weeks by the Forest Department. The fish were not biting and the newness had gone away. All four boys were now ready to pan for gold. I showed them how to get gravel from around large rocks. At that time I had four gold pans so each boy could search where ever they chose.

About an hour later they had had it. They were tired of panning and not getting anything. We had supper and had built a large bonfire where of the kids played in. Around eight o'clock in the evening I told the boys that we should take the sluice box and put it in the water and build a dam so there would be a good flow of water the box.

Before I had finished speaking the boys were up and dragging the sluice box down to the stream bed. It was fun watching them as they formed a dam and soon have about four inches of water running through the sluice box.

With that done the boys decided that they wanted to shovel some gravel and sand into the box to see how it worked. We didn't have enough shovels for all four but the two without shovels soon found other implements to assist in digging.

By this time it was completely dark so I got the gas powered lamp and soon had it going. I sit the lantern up on the creek bank as it was about five foot high at that place on the creek. The boys were making the gravel fly as each wanted to put the most gravel.

Ten o'clock came and went and those boys were still shoveling like crazy. At a little after eleven o'clock I called a halt to the mining operation and told the boys it was time to call it quits and time for bed. They had put in a hard three hours of shoveling and were soon fast asleep.

Early the next morning the boys were eager to get breakfast over with and get back to their gold hunting. Once again the gravel and sand were flying. It is not really a good place to be searching for gold, but it was so close to the campsite the boys could have cared less.

Around noon I convinced the boys that they should stop and take a look at what might be in the sluice box. This meant that the sluice box would have to be raised enough to cut down on the water flow through it.

Finally the remaining large rock and white sand had been cleaned away. Now it was time to divide the black sand into four pans so each boy could work it around to see if there was any gold in the bottom of their pans.

Slowly, very slowly the black sand was washed around in all pans. There were some small pieces of gold but it is what I called flour gold. The pieces were so small that they could not be picked up with tweezers. All of the black sand and gold was put in a large can to take home where I would put one drop of mercury into the pan with the black sand and flour gold. The pan was swirled around until the mercury was hard and could be picked with fingers or tweezers.

The boys had a good time and enjoyed their midnight gold panning. Soon the weekend came to a close and we had to head for home. All four boys wanted to go back and try their hand again in gold panning.

Some where I still have a small bottle with hard balls of mercury in it. I have another bottle holding the large piece of gold I found.

There were many stories of gold panning and I must add that the preacher of our church wanted to go to the gold country and try his hand at gold panning. Arrangements were made and a date set for another treck to Bull Creek.

Pastor Melton and his family had brought a large pull camper and were set up in the small clearing that we normally set up camp. The road down into the meadow was too steep and rough for them to try getting the camper where were camped.

Early Saturday morning Melton was up and ready to try gold panning. I decided to take him up the small creek that flowed into Bull Creek. I had always found gold there but it was mainly the flour gold stuff. Going about one hundred feet up the small stream the creek bed was really narrow the steep sloping sides were bed rock and the stream was only about two feet wide at that point. There was a rather large piece of rock sitting right in the middle of the stream.

I had never panned around that specific spot so I decided that it would be a good site to start at. We dug out as much sand and gravel as we could with out moving the rock. I don't know why but I decided to remove the rock and finish filling up the gold pan with what was under the rock.

We had a full gold pan and it was difficult to get started working the gravel and sand around in the pan. After much trial and error between the two of us we were down to just black sand in the pan. I demonstrated how the water was to be run around the pan and move just a small amount of the black sand each time the water went around the pan. With just a little movement there were specks of gold. We stopped counting when the count got over one hundred. This was the most gold I had ever found or seen in one pan of gravel.

The gold and black sand was placed in a small bottle and we were off to search out another spot that had been overlooked. We did find more gold but once again it was all the very small pieces, flour gold. It does not take long to get tired of working the gold pan and to day was not exception. Melton and I were both tired and soon decided that we had had enough for one day.

Melton and family left Saturday evening and headed back to Vallejo as he was to preach the next morning service.

During our trips to the mountains and camping on Bull Creek during one of our many motorcycle rides, we found two old abandoned houses. They were small but on different outing we stayed in both of them at different times. One such trip involved several of the men that I worked with. We sit up camp in the building and all spread our sleeping bags around an old barrel stove. The weather was cold enough that a fire during the evening and night was a comfort. During the day we rode motorcycles all about.

On another winter outing we decided to stay in the larger of the two cabins. Dan took his truck as well as the truck and camper I had. The ground was frozen so we didn't have any trouble getting in and out. It was just after Christmas and a New Year trip was planned.

Once again there was a large drum stove and we had a nice time camping in the building. Of course there were the many barking spiders that always seem to go where ever there are people.

It was New Years Eve and we had had a large camp fire built out side so marshmallows were cooked as well as keep warm. When midnight approached everyone soon found a pan or bucket or something to beat on and make noise. At midnight there was much shouting and beating on what ever one had. It was a good celebration and the kids enjoyed the time of fun as the New Year was ushered in.

Joy and Dad sat out by the fire long after the celebrating had ended. Much to my surprise that is when the two become interested in each other.

In later years Joy, when asked how she met Dan would say "my daddy brought him home for me" They have now been married over thirty years and looking forward to many more years together.

LIFE IS SO SHORT

There are those that don't know it
Time moves so swiftly
Stop to smell the roses
Take the time to look about

Look at a tree and admire its beauty
Listen to the birds as they sing
Spend a moment to listen to nature
Creatures as they scurry about

Can you spare the time?
To care about someone else?
Say a word of kindness
Ask about their life

Listen and not worry about yours
Give them the attention you want
It will return a thousand fold
With Blessings untold.

Be thankful for each morning
Thankful that your eyes open
Ears that can hear
And voice to share with others

Stop and listen to your heartbeat
Look at the beauties that abound
As the day begins to unwind.
Be thankful that you can

MOVING TO NORFOLK

In early nineteen fifty eight I was out of work. I had tried every possible means of getting a job. As my last recourse I contacted the local navy recruiter about going back into the navy.

I could enlist for a four year term and, but I had to go back to being an airman at the pay grade of E 3, I was an E 4 when I got out of the navy in nineteen fifty four. I was told that I would be assigned to the same classification field of simulators as I was when I had left the navy in nineteen fifty four.

I was desperate since I had a family to now consider, a wife and three children. Finally I signed the papers and awaited orders of where I would report.

A week later the orders came in and I was being assigned to the naval station at Key West, Florida. Not where I thought I would be assigned but beggars can't be choosey. I was told that I would be attending Sonabuoy School. At that time I did not think much about it and never questioned if I would be able to pursue a career in the field of flight simulators, I had worked in before, while in the navy. I wanted to work in the field of flight simulators which at the time was the Tradevman rating.

I was given a first class ticket for the flight to Key West. I had never been assigned a seat in first class before. It was a pleasant flight and I was soon in Key West, Florida. Transportation was provided to the naval base and I was checked into the transit barracks. This is a building where one could live until assigned to their regular quarters.

I had my original issue of clothing. A complete sea bag I brought with me. Upon checking in I was told that I would be reissued a complete set of clothing. Wonderful, now I had two sea bags of clothing to take care of.

After being there for four days I went to the personnel office and explained to the officer that I wanted to strike for the Tradevman rating. To my surprise I found a listening ear to explain my predicament to. He told me he would send a letter to the headquarters of personnel and explains that I had been told by the recruiter that I could work in the field as I did when I was on active duty before.

Three days later a reply came back and agreed to my wanting to work in the field of flight simulators. I would be receiving orders to a new duty station in a few days. Sure enough I received orders to the naval air station at Norfolk Naval Air station. In three weeks I would be transferred.

In the mean time I had no job to do and it made for very long days to while away the hours. One morning I was asked if I would be in charge of the coffee mess until I was shipped out. I agreed, it was not a glamorous job but it did fill my days.

I had to report to work each morning at five o'clock and get the crew that was assigned, mustered; taking roll call is what it amounted to. There were donuts and other sweets to sell along with the coffee. Some times we could not keep up with the demand for coffee. All the while I sat at the head of the line and collected money for what was purchased.

The coffee mess made money while I was in charge, something that had not occurred in the past. Still I was put in charge and I wanted to get off on the right foot with the personnel department.

Finally the time passed and I boarded a plane not to Norfolk Virginia but to Bloomington Indiana. I exchanged my ticket as I planned to fly to Bloomington and pack up my family to move to Norfolk.

It was a rushed packing job, I had a small trailer to pull and we planned to take as much as possible with us to this new assignment.

114

The day arrived that we had to start our trip to Norfolk. The kids were excited, I was excited and I had the feeling that my wife was excited as well.

That night I drove far into the night, finally stopping for a few hours of sleep then continuing our journey. Arriving at Norfolk in the late afternoon we had no place to stay the night. Did not have enough money to get a motel room. Finally we found an apartment complex abut three miles from the base. It is now approaching four o'clock in the afternoon. I went into the office and inquired in there was an apartment that I could rent. I was told that yes, there were empty quarters and if I would sign a one year lease I could have the apartment that evening.

I sure hated to sign a one year lease but I was desperate for a roof over our heads. My wife was upset at the fact that I had signed the papers and had not even looked at the apartment. We stayed in the apartment the next night. I checked into the department called FATULANT. Actually this stands for Fleet Aviation Training Unit Atlantic Fleet. There is a similar unit on the west coast, FATUPAC, Fleet Aviation Training Unit Training Unit Pacific. Later in my career I was assigned to this unit when I was assigned to Lemoore California FATUPAC DETACHMENT LEMOORE but that was later in my naval career, which is another story.

At Norfolk I was assigned to the FATU PAC detachment ASW department. This is aviation anti-submarine warfare training. In another part of this book I have described what I did while stationed there.

After the year lease was up my family and I rented a house where we could feel more like a family in a regular home. It was a welcome change; all of the rooms were on the same floor. In the apartment all of the bedrooms were up stairs.

We did have some problems like our son got up one night and fell down the stairs. Was not hurt badly so we were fortune in that respect.

115

I still have memories of our youngest child. She was not able to walk up right going up or down the stairs. Coming down she would sit down and sort of slide down the steps. She would have the biggest smile as she descended. Smile that I have never forgotten. Cute, that only a father would remember.

We lived in the rented home for about two years, and then we decided to buy a home using the GI Bill to help us get into the home.

All told we lived at Norfolk for five years. Enjoyed, traveling up and down the east coast, visiting all of the historic sites. Our children were young and do not remember most of them.

I requested to be sent to the navy "B" school for what I wanted was advance training in the simulation field. Little did I know that I had stated the request incorrectly. Instead of being assigned to the school as a student, I was assigned to the school as a member of the Tradevman Training staff. Elsewhere I have written about this assignment else where in this book.

I did learn a very valuable lesson, think long and hard how you make a request. Read it many times and them ask some one else to read it and make sure it is stated correctly. I was fortune in that having to teach through all of the phases of both the "A" and "B" schools. This way the information was ingrained and was a great help in my making the advancement to Chief Petty Office later.

SNOW SKIING

Snow skiing is one sport that I never thought I would be interested in doing. However when I was sixty three years old my youngest daughter Suzi talked me into trying it. I was very skeptical about the whole thing.

Who in the whole wide world would want to strap two boards on their feet and slide down a hillside? I didn't know what a bunny slope was either. I rented skis and boots at the local shop and the skis were adjusted to break free with just a small amount of force. Good, as I was sure I would be falling many times during the day! I just didn't know how many times I would find myself face down in the snow.

On my first time to the snow it was decided that I would take the morning beginners class! I showed up with a whole bunch of other people that didn't know how to ski either. There were really young people and, a lot of people in their middle years. To no ones surprise I was the oldest person in the class.

Let me start by saying I have never worked so hard at any thing in my whole life. First we had to learn to walk up a slight incline. It is not easy task. First you turn the skis outward as far as you can. Then you try to lift up one ski and place it forward up the slope. Then comes the other ski and it is lifted up and placed forward up the slope. Nothing to it, right? That is right; there is nothing to it—NOT!! It is almost impossible. I struggled and struggled and finally made an advance of about ten feet.

Next we were placed in two lines about six feet apart on the same slope. When the instructor pointed to you, you walked, make that waddled forward and then sorta made a jump turning you facing down hill. A person's weight and the slick snow let you glide slowly down the hill.

We did many other things but I have not told about the hardest parts. I have not even begun to tell you about the hardest parts, they were still to come.

Next we were lined up at the chair lift to take us to the top of the bunny slope. Then it came my turn for me and another person to slide clumsily in front of the chair, all the while holding on to two ski poles. I barely made it and my partner for the up the trip barely made it as well. It is pretty as the cable moves along slowly toward the top of the hill.

Wait a minute there is the part about getting off the chair at the top of the hill. I was terrified because first of all I had never had to jump out of a moving chair. Keep the ski tips up as you approach the jump off point. Try not to spear the other person with you. I was sitting on the right side of the lift chair. I would try to go straight ahead and then turn to the right if possible. I was not too good at turning on the beginners slope. Surely I can glide straight ahead and try not to trip myself in the process.

Almost to the top and now I am nervous. Hands sweating, in spite of the cold. Inside my ski pants and jacket I was sweating as well, it sure is hard work learning to ski.

Almost there and I lean forward so my weight will be over my skis when the time comes. Almost—almost—time to push off and be back on the snow. Wheeee, I am sliding forward, and I start to congratulate myself when—zip my skis stopped and I didn't, plowing my face into the snow before I can get my arms out in front of me. I looked around to see if anyone was laughing at me, none were and I quickly regained my feet, err make that my skis. I waddle off to await the whole group to make it to the top. Many more people fell but there was not one laugh in the whole group.

The instructor counted and when all were accounted for we were formed into single file. The instructor started off leading and made slow gentle turns. Hey this is not too bad! We were going back and forth across the across the gentle slope. It was a matter of shifting ones weight to the down hill side and then standing up straight when you want to go straight ahead. Everything was going pretty good as long as the slope did not increase. But it did increase the farther we traveled downward.

Now it is even harder to shift ones weight when the slope increases. But we made it down the hill without anyone falling. I thought I would fall a thousand times. There were times of almost falling but with wild swinging of ones arms I was able to regain control. I am sure there were people watching and having a good laugh at the beginners on the bunny slope.

I am time for a rest!! Big time rest!! The class is over and it is time for lunch and rest the weary legs. It is strange that one can work up a tremendous appetite with just skiing.

After lunch I felt more like going back to the lift and giving the bunny slope, another try. Off we go and this time I had much less trouble getting in the lift chair. The ride up the hill is so peaceful and quite. You can watch others going down the hill. Some are flying and some are slower and some are just down right slow. That is my class, SLOW!

This time I had less trouble getting off at the top. Resting as the rest of our group arrives. There is Suzi, Andrew, Matt and I in our group. Now it is time to start the descent. The boys race ahead and are gleefully encouraging each other to try something different. Me I just carefully ski across the slope and make a one eighty and go back across the slope. All the while we are getting closer to the middle of the hill. It is a little steeper now and I am having trouble getting my weight transferred to the down hill ski. Oh no! I can't get the skis to turn and I am headed straight down the hill. Well almost, actually I am headed directly toward a very large pine tree. What to do?? It flashed through my mind that I would be skiing directly to the tree; I couldn't get the skis to turn. Faster and faster I am going and I am for sure now that there is a large pine tree in my future.

I am only about fifteen feet from the tree when I decided that I would just fall down and—and what? Down I go on my back and swiftly I am now sliding on my back with my head pointed toward the tree. One ski came off and I spread my arms and legs to slow my momentum. I am just about stopped when I feel my head and shoulders drop into the deep depression where no snow has fallen. Completely around the tree there is an area about eighteen inches out from the tree that is also about eighteen inches deep. My head and shoulders were in that depression. My feet are pointed toward the sky. I can't move!! I can't get up!!

Well I just laid there and began to laugh. The more I thought about the situation, that I could not help myself, it was just funny! The more I thought about it the more I laughed. Soon I hear voices and Suzi asking if I was hurt!

The only thing hurt was my pride! How would you feel if you could not move and laughing so hard it that was taken for cries of pain??

It took the two boys and Suzi to pull me up out of hole. They had found my ski and were giving encouragement to jump back on the skis and continue on down the hill. I must tell you I stayed far away from the tree line the rest of the day.

After the third or fourth time going down the bunny slope Suzi wanted to go on a different run. I was hesitant but all three were positive that the one they wanted to try was not any more difficult than the bunny slope.

Off we go to a different chair lift. This time going up took longer and it was so peaceful and quiet, it is amazing how one spirits can be lifted up viewing the beautiful country side all covered with more than five feet of snow, we were some thirty feet above the ground. Every once in a while we would see someone's gloves or a jacket or even a ski pole.

Arriving at the top was breath taking; it was such a beautiful view from the top of the mountain. Once we were all together it was time to start down. We were on a road and the path was wide enough for several people to pass on either side.

What I found disconcerting at first is that you would hear someone yell "on your right" then the person would pass at a much greater speed than I was going. After a few such incidents it was nice to be warned of someone passing.

I just say that I did have several places where I fell. Never going fast, I just couldn't get the skis to turn when I wanted them to turn.

Suzi and the boys were just ahead of me and they had stopped to let me catch up. I have not told yet of what is done to stop. Actually the tips of the skis are both pointed inward so the skis for the bottom of a "V". It sounds easy and I had had some limited success. When I say limited I mean I was only successful about half of the time.

I am coming up to a wide spot that Suzi and the boys were standing. I put on the "V" and didn't slow down before I reached them. Bang, I run into all three and we all were lying on the snow. I apologized profusely but they were laughing so hard that I am sure they didn't hear a word.

We got back to our feet and off we went down the winding and slippery slope. Finally arriving at the foot of the mountain, I was ready to try it again. Surely I MIGHT make it down the hill with out falling.

We tried several different trails that day. I was getting a little better the more I skied. At about three o'clock it was decided that we all had had enough skiing for one day and off came the skis and strapped then on the carrier on the roof top.

Once in the car I realized just how tired I am. Who in the world would pay to work so hard? On the way home I declared that I was never going skiing again. It just was not worth all the work and effort.

I made that statement and surely I would stick with my word. Wrong!!

After arriving home and taking a long leisurely bath. I felt much better. In fact I told my wife that I was ready to go skiing again. Suzi laughed when I informed her that I was ready to go again. I could hardly wait until for the next trip to the snow.

We skied many different ski resorts that year. Sugar bowl is the one I can remember the name. I had one place that I liked better than the others; Suzi will have to tell me the name as I can't remember it today.

SPECIAL TIMES

I am about twelve or thirteen years old and was preparing for another day at school. It was nothing special and I was taking my time getting ready.

Dad walked into the house and I asked why he was home and not at work? Dad said that he took the day off from work and was going to Indianapolis to look at some used surplus military transmitters and receivers that he was interested in.

The idea sprang forth that if dad was taking the day off from work maybe he would let me skip school and go with him. I put the question to him and to my surprise he agreed.

Wonders of wonders I would get to spend the day with dad. We were soon in the nineteen thirty model A and on our way.

Dad never drove fast and today was no exception. Forty five miles per hour was as fast as we ever achieved. I did not care, I had the whole day to be dad. Something that did not occur often, except on the weekends.

I enjoy the ride to Indianapolis though there were few words between us. Dad did not have to talk to communicate to me. The few words that were spoken were about school. Since I was one of those kids that studied little or none, there was not much conversation on that subject.

We arrived in Indianapolis and dad was soon engrossed in going thought piles and piles of surplus radio gear. He knew what he was looking for. I did know and was of little use to him except to keep the stuff he wanted in a separate pile.

It didn't take dad long to find what he wanted. He paid the price asked and them we carried the boxes out to the car.

Placing them carefully in the back seat of the car we were soon on our way home.

Once again there was not much conversation on the way home. I guess dad was going over the equipment in his mind and what all would be entailed in converting them to operate on the voltages common to his power supplies.

He showed me when we got home what he would have to do and all of the work that would be necessary to convert from military aircraft power and what was available in dad's shop.

I am very proud of my father. He was self taught in electronics. I know he had an electronic text book and had studied it to learn what he needed to know.

When I was about fifteen Dad undertook to teach me about electronics. I attended night school with him after he was hired at RCA as a troubleshooter.

Sorry to say not much sunk in until later in life. When I joined the navy and was assigned to the link shack my limited studies helped. Later in life I set about to learn electronics to a higher level.

While teaching at Memphis in the basic and advanced school TV was an area that was completely engulfing. I worked hard to stay ahead of the lessons I was assigned to teach. I would learn the subject and then teach it to the class. What a learning experience it was.

All of this I must give my father credit for starting me into the field of electronics at an early age

THE STORY OF YESTERYEAR

Yesteryear is not a word, it is not recognized as such in our language.
Yet it does have a ring about it that sings in my heart.
I know because I am a part of yesteryear.
We each feel it with the passing of years.
Watch someone you call old.

Consider the young woman walking down the street.
Look upon the continence of a child just born.
Can you see what it will be in twenty or forty years?
No we do not look at life that way! We do not see what lies ahead.
Yet look at someone you consider old, what do you see?

Is there a yesteryear in the comparison?
Surely there must be!
Hope springs eternal within our breasts
With each passing glance!
Can you see where it lies or what it used to be?

Yesteryear is there for all to see. What each wants it to be!
It is for each of us to make that determination!

STUDEBAKER COUPE

My family and I were transferred to the Norfolk Naval Air Station in nineteen fifty eight. For the first year we lived in an apartment building and did not like it at all. When we arrived in Norfolk we needed a place to live quickly. I signed a one year lease when I found the home was vacant and that we could move what little belongs we had carried from Indiana. Still it was a roof over our heads and a place we could call home.

After the years lease was up we rented a three bedroom house. It was a corner lot so the three children had a yard to play in. About a year later my wife saw a large garage being moved somewhere down the street. We located the home and garage, later and there was a for sale sign in the front yard.

Evidently we were interested in the house because it had three bedrooms. There were hardwood oak floors in the living area and the dinning area. We started the paper work to purchase the house on the GI bill. Nothing down and small monthly payments.

One of the first things I did was rent a floor sander and resurfaced all of the hardwood floors. It was a lot of work but than again I was young and felt that I could make the flooring look so much better after sanding and varnishing the flooring.

About six weeks later we moved into the home and just fell in love with it. My wife had a house she could call her own and I had a large garage in the back yard.

After getting settled in I had the task of removing a very large tree stump that set just between the house and garage. I dug, and dug, and them dug more. Finally I had a hole about six feet in diameter. It was slow going because of all the roots that had to be exposed and chopped

126

off. When it was done I hooked the Studebaker to the stump and pulled the stump enough to break the tap root.

I must go back and explain how I come to own the Studebaker car in the first place. A young man I worked with had recently married and when he moved his wife to the Norfolk area he bought the nineteen fifty two door sedan for his move.

About three weeks after buying the car he and his wife decided one Saturday morning to visit the naval commissary to purchase food. While driving toward the commissary his wife tossed a cigarette out the right side window. Unbeknown to her the cigarette did not go outside the car. Instead it had blown back into the rear seat of the car.

They parked and proceeded into the commissary and started shopping. Suddenly there was an announcement on the speaker system that there was a red car in the parking area on fire. Not knowing if it was their car they quickly left the store and sure enough it was their car that was on fire. The fire was contained in the rear seat and quickly put out by the base fire department.

The car was not drivable because the rear and side windows were broken. The front seat was burned on the back. Everything inside the car had black smoke on it. The car was towed to a local towing yard.

Monday arriving at work the young man told of how his car burned up. He was now out of transportation! I asked if I could go with him to look at the car. He was more than willing and we left at lunch time to view the car. It was a beautiful off red color and the outside was all good except for the roof area over the back seat. All of the paint had been burned away. In fact the roof area had started to rust.

I asked Joe what he would take for the car! I could see that little Studebaker champion coupe fixed up and back on the road. At first Joe said he would like to have thirty dollars for the car to pay off the tow truck company.

I told him I would have to think about it and discuss it with my wife. The next day Joe came up to me right after morning muster. He had talked with his wife and told me that they really needed a washing machine. They would take a washing machine instead of money. I agreed and could hardly wait to go home and share this information with my wife. She grabbed the morning paper and there was a washing machine for sale a few blocks away. We called to make an appointment for that same afternoon.

Arriving at the house in a rain storm I waited a few minutes before getting out of the car. The rain quickly stopped and I opened the car door and walked around back of the car. Looking down at the water in the gutter I spotted what looked like a dollar bill floating toward me. I reached down and retrieved the bill. To my surprise it was a twenty dollar bill. It had been delivered to me from the heavens above.

Upon inspecting the washing machine I asked what they were asking for it. Much to my surprise they wanted twenty dollars for the washing machine. I quickly agreed and handed the lady the twenty dollar bill I had found a few minutes before. The machine was quickly loaded into our station wagon and we were off to make the delivery to Joe and his wife.

The next day was Saturday and I make arrangements to drive the little Studebaker coupe home. I took some cardboard to place on the driver's seat and we were soon on our way home.

I was so proud of that little car; it had a rakish look to its body shape. Upon arriving home I wasted no time in getting all of the burnt seats out. The side panel's front and rear were beyond repair so they came out as well. Soon the whole interior was removed. The steering wheel and the front dash were all still in good shape. None of the electrical wiring had been damaged.

Now it was time to search the local junk yards for all of the parts I would need to restore the car to its original condition. Windows, seats and door panels were soon in my garage and ready to be installed. But before doing the inside I wanted to start on repairing the roof.

I sanded the inside as well as the out side, taking it down to shiny metal. Did not take long to do that. Next I decided that the top was to be an off white color down to the door window line.

The top was masked off so that there would not be overspray on the rest of the car. Soon primer paint was on and a nice white paint was applied over the primer.

Three days later rust came through the paint in an area where the heat was the hottest. Soon the area was sanded and once more a heavy coat of primer as applied. This time I did not put the final coat on as I wanted to see if the rust would come through. Well it did and now I was at a loss as what to do and where to start searching for a paint that would not let the rust through. This was in the days before rust proof paint. I traveled to several paint stores and asked for anything that would prevent the rust from coming through.

Finally found a shop that had an acid wash that was to be applied to the metal before any paint was applied. There was a stipulation that the acid wash had to dry for three days before applying paint to the surface.

Guess what, it worked and I finally had a beautiful white top on the car. Next I started on the interior and within a months time I had a fine car to drive to work and the best part is that it got much better gas mileage. We had a nineteen fifty seven Chevy station wagon painted in the standard blue and white.

I drove the car to work every day and really loved that little Studebaker coupe. It was so easy to get around in traffic. The only thing was it was a stick shift and my wife didn't do shifting.

We received orders to Memphis Tennessee in nineteen sixty two. I already had a trailer to haul the items that we would need. I left my wife and children with my mother as there was still six weeks of the school for the kids to finish. I drove on to Memphis checked in and then started looking for a house for the family.

I found a lovely three bedroom house for rent about two miles west of the base. It was out in the country and there was a very large yard for the children to play. It took three weeks of cleaning and washing to get the house ready to live in. I had our household furnishing delivered and every thing was ready for the family to move in.

I rode a Grey Hound bus to mother's house one Friday evening. Arriving late in the night I didn't was to wake the children as we would be leaving the next day to travel to Memphis.

The trailer we had towed from Norfolk was already packed and I hitched it to the fifty seven Chevy and we were off to our new home. The kids were excited to see their new home. I was anxious to have them all together with me once more.

After serving four years at Memphis I once again received orders to a new duty station. Naval Air Station Lemoore, California was to be our next assignment.

I had already purchased a new Chevy truck and camper. The fifty seven Chevy was getting a lot of miles on it and I really did not want to start across country in it, so it was sold and of all things the young man that bought it came to me a week later and asked if I thought it would make the trip across country to California? Sure as long as you check the oil frequently and don't let it over heat. Never hear any more from him so I have to assume that it make the trip just fine.

Now came the hard part, I decided to sell the little Studebaker coupe as well. It was just not feasible to drive two vehicles across country. I was sorry that it was gone. Many times I wish I had kept it. I still do today

THE BAD GUY

It is a beautiful spring day. Out in town doing some shopping. We bought some of this and some of that. As usual we had been all over the west side of town. The weather was beautiful in the sixties almost shirt sleeve weather.

There I was, minding my own business. I wasn't bothering anyone! I wasn't looking for trouble, nor did I expect any.

I had just ordered my favorite sandwich, fries and a drink. Carrying them to my table, I was looking forward to a pleasant meal.

Looking around there was not a lot of people in the restaurant as I unwrapped my sandwich. Slowly turning back the wrapper, I am ready to pick it up and take the first bite.

Slowly I take a bite, and shift it to the right side of my mouth. As my teeth came together there is a sudden sharp pain in the tooth second from the back on the right lower jaw.

Whoopee that was really a high level pain. What is wrong with that tooth? I wanted to ask, but a tooth can not answer back.

Slowly I shift the food to the left side and began to chew. There was no pain on the left side. I continued to consume the hamburger.

Little did I know at that time that the pain was to get worse.

Last week I was putting stuff in the truck to go to Letha's to get some yard plants to plant around my home. The wind made it feel very cold, like about 10 degrees.

I started to have pain in the right side of my neck. But I still went ahead with what I was doing. By the time we were in the truck and headed down to Letha's house all of the teeth on the right side of my mouth started to ache.

After the truck warmed up inside, the pain started to go away. When we got out at Letha's and in the wind, again the pain came back, just as bad as before. We got one tree to plant in our back yard and headed for home, as I couldn't take it any more.

The general pain stopped but one tooth still had an ache. By Thursday I wanted that tooth out really bad. Made an appointment for the next day, to see the dentist that made my wife's bite plate for cancer radiation treatments.

The bite plate fits the upper jaw very, very tight. There is about a six inch extention from the teeth mold. The bite plate handle is bolted to a "U" shaped device which in turn is bolted to the seat back. It is designed to hold the head in the same position day after day for the radiation treatments.

Now back to the dentist, after examining the x-ray of the tooth, he said that there was infection around the roots of the tooth and that it needed to be extracted. I was all prepared to have the tooth pulled right then and there. The dentist informs me that he does not do extractions. He would send me to an oral surgeon

To make a long story short and seeing two different dentists the tooth was out and the intense pain was gone.

I have not had any amount of tooth pain for a number of years. This was a reminder that when one "gets" infected, it can go fast and does cause lots of pain.

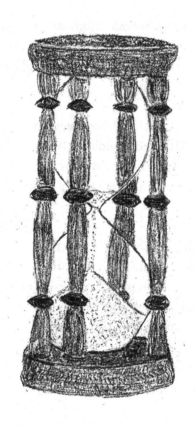

TIME

Once it was only the quickness of minutes. Those
followed by quickness of days. Till now it is the
years that flow as water, so quickly.

Wish one could stop the passage of time, for it flows
all too quickly. When once I was but a small child,
now the reference of old has me in its grasp.

Some, when asked if they would like to live life over again
respond with a quick no and a bitter smile on their lips.

No, so say I too, for I would live it again and again
until I finally have it right. As many trips as possible,
even if I had to start afresh, each time.

But it is no use, wish as I may; there is no turning back, no repeats
that is known. As a child it seems like life goes on forever. Days are
sooo long and time passes sooo slowly. Oh, for those days again when
there were no worries, no concerns, except for eating and sleeping.

Even as a teenager I was anxious to be older. To drive a car!! To
be out of school!! Wanting a job!! Earn money to buy what, really
did not know! I just knew that every fact of life required money.

Later, I wanted to be a part of a great effort to set
the world on fire. To be known and praised!!

A time of comfort as I realize that I will never achieve
greatness. Not even a little flame. But, who cares?

Now as the days slip by faster and faster, I want to set the
clock back, to slow down. For the days flow so swiftly. Now I
know the dread. For it is coming and is one ever prepared?

Water Skiing in a Bayou

My family and I were stationed at the Memphis Naval Air Station when I received orders that I would be transferred to the Mine Warfare School. It was always nice to know that every four years or so I would be moving to another duty assignment.

I had traded a go-kart for a motorcycle which I then traded for a sixteen foot motorboat. We had bent the rear axle on the go-kart and I had purchased a new one but had not got around to making the repair.

One of sailors I worked with wanted the go-kart and had a motorcycle. I didn't really want the motorcycle but I knew another sailor that wanted the motorcycle and had a boat that he would trade.

I had the motorcycle for two days and then made the swap. Actually the boat was not in too bad of shape. But the motor had a blown head gasket. Knowing I could likely repair the engine I went ahead with the deal. I had to replace one piston and rings and then put it back together.

Actually a really easy job, the hardest part was locating a dealer to purchase the parts. Had to make two trips to down town Memphis, when I finally purchased the necessary parts. After the repairs the engine started easy and ran good. It did not have an electric starting motor; rather it had a pull rope. Seldom did it fail to start on the second pull. I tried it out on the Mississippi river. The river is so big and the current is so swift I was fearful the whole time.

We made many trips to Sardis campground, which was about an hour and a half drive south of Memphis. I can't remember the name of the river but there was a large camping ground and we introduced all of our camping friends to the place.

Upon receiving orders to Charleston we made plans to include the boat. It was still in good shape and we could put about anything inside the boat while going cross country. Actually we towed the boat to the Bloomington area and spent many days playing in the waters of Lake Monroe.

Upon arriving at Charleston we applied for navy housing and were told that a house would be available in three days. It was brand new housing and we were so happy to learn of the quickness of the house being available. Soon our household goods were delivered and we once again had a home.

The back side of our house was toward a bayou of water which eventually ran into the St. Lawrence River. We took the boat where the two met and water skied there many times.

It was not before I asked my son Steve if he wanted to see how far up the bayou we could go. He agreed and off we went, it is about three miles to our house and I didn't know if Steve wanted to go that far with out stopping for a break.

We made it just fine and actually turned around right behind our house. What we later learned, that there are many water snakes which live in the bayou. We learned of this fact later.

We make many fishing trips up the bayou and fished next to a water pumping station about two blocks from our back yard. We caught many blue gill fish which my wife really enjoyed. Steve and I fished all over the place. One time we had gone up the St. Lawrence about five miles and the water was very high. We went through an opening in a dike when we discovered that we were actually trying to fish in a rice field. The water was not deep and the motor started to kick up when it would make contact with the bottom. We shut the engine down and I used a paddle to get up back out into the main channel of the river. We never caught any fish in the big river but still had a good time being together. We had many good hours together.

It was while we were at Charleston that Steve was old enough to get his driving permit. It was on the road to where the two rivers met that we spent many hours letting him practice all of the maneuvers that he would have to face while driving. We practiced with both the automatic transmission and with the stick shift. I think he learned quickly and became a fine driver.

We visited some of the most beautiful gardens around the Charleston area. The azalea gardens are wonderful with the large trees and the hanging moss. I couldn't begin to describe he beauty. It is something that one must experience for themselves.

While at the Mine Warfare School I received notification that I had been selected for advancement to Chief Petty Officer. Those four long years at Memphis had finally paid off. It was an honor to be selected and I eagerly waited the official date that I would be advanced.

There is always a special party at the E-7 club when new members are welcomed into their new rating. I started the day off in my completely new chief's uniform. It is a drastic change when going from an E-6 to an E-7.

The party started when I first arrived at work. I think every E-7 in the whole school showed up demanding that I shine their shoes. I never shined so many shoes in my whole life and I had shined a lot from boot camp on up to the present. It was always necessary that ones shoes have a spit shine everyday.

It was just about time for the party at the chiefs club when half dozen chiefs showed at my office. They took my chiefs hat completely apart and scattered the parts all around the office. Being new at the art of assembling a chief's hat it took much long than usual to get it all back together.

All of the new selectee's had been instructed to bring a working set of kaki clothes for the celebration party. After arriving at the club and seeing what the new chiefs had to do, I was glad that I had the work uniform.

I was the only airman at the party; my rating is part of the aviation branch of the navy, all the rest were in what we called the back shoe navy. My uniform required that I wear brown shoes and the sea going branch wore black shoes. My brown shoes got me into many unusual events during the party. Since I was in the air branch of the navy I had to act like an airplane whenever I was called to serve someone. The only disgusting part of the party for me was that I had to stand in a trash can and drink some horrible concoction that was made from every conceivable liquid that is used in a kitchen, to this was added two raw eggs. I got the eggs down, down several times in fact. I would swallow them and they would imminently come right back up into the cup. I never did get them to stay down. They eventually wound up at the bottom of the trash can.

At three o'clock the party ended and each new chief was called forward for the swearing in oath. It was a somber ceremony and each of us accepted the advancement with pride. I was proud to be a chief petty officer. I am still proud today that I served many years in the navy. I learned a lot, I learned how to lead men. I learned that it is a privilege to serve in the United States Navy.

Every person being advanced was required to put their money for advancement uniforms in the kitty to pay for the party. When the party was over we did get most of our money back.

I would go back and do it all over again.

THINKING OF YOU

Where does it all begin?
Romance has so many places
Of when you came into my life
The beautiful young woman
That captured my heart

Teasing you to get your attention
Pulling your hair
Am I getting through?
Will she see me
As I look from afar?

Touching your beautiful hair
Trying to hold your hand
Or catch your eye
Will she like me?
My mind asks again and again

To sit next to you
To put my arm around you
Slip close and let our shoulders touch
There, I did it! A thrill runs up my back
Ah! She likes me from the smile she flashed!

SECTION III

FLYING

FLYING
PART I

I have loved flying since I was old enough to understand what an airplane was. My first flight when I was only five years old. I shall never forget the thrill of that first plane ride.

I have written about my experience and how scared I was and that I might fall right out of the airplane. When I was allowed to take the controls and not knowing, I moved the control stick quickly to the left. Causing concern, both from the pilot, and from Dad! Then after an explanation from the pilot, I quickly learned that all that was required was a gentle pressure applied to the stick. My first lesson!

I was so proud that I had been allowed to control the airplane even if it was just for a few fleeting seconds. It was burned into my brain. I dreamed of flying over our farm and waving to Mother and Dad on the ground below somewhere. Of being able to gracefully move the airplane where I wanted it to go. Little did I realize that it would be many years before I would actually receive flight instructions and earn my private pilots license. I was over forty years old before it would come about.

I joined the Navy in 1950 to keep from being drafted into the army. I knew that I would much rather live aboard a ship, have a bed and receive three hot meals a day. The army lets you dig a foxhole and sleep in it. Good weather or bad, hot or cold and then there is the rain to think about. At the time it did not seem like much of a chose to sleep inside or out in the mud and dirt that seems to become the standard issue for someone in the army.

Having talked to the navy recruiters I was assured that I qualified for the air branch of the navy. I scored high in aviation, mechanics, math and English. Good enough that I thought I would not get a draft notice.

After getting a phone call from the recruiter in July that it was only a matter of a few days and I would be getting a draft notice. I agreed that it seemed best that I agree to sign papers making it official.

Arrangements were made for transportation to Great Lakes Training Center. I and many other young men were off to begin our recruit training. We were scheduled to have twelve weeks of intensive training.

Due to the rapid development of the Korean War our training was shortened to about ten weeks. Sailors were needed, quickly to man all of the ships that were required. Leaving the Great Lakes Training Center, two days, before Thanksgiving. Our train arrived around midnight at Pensacola Florida just before thanksgiving. Transported to temporary quarters and given bedding and assigned to a bunk.

All of us arose early Thanksgiving Day thanks to the early morning schedule we had while in boot camp. Each day began at five a.m. there.

We milled about smartly not knowing where the chow hall was located. We had not had dinner the evening before due to our late arrival time. Everyone was eager to get some food. We were told to assemble outside and would be off to the chow hall. Little did I know I was to get a rude awaking when we finally started through the actual food line.

The very first thing that was put on my metal tray was hard navy beans. They plinked on the metal as each bean touched the tray. I don't remember much else about what we were given to eat except bread with all the butter we wanted and, this is the best part of the meal, the milk was icy cold. There you have it, a man of the world and the first meal out of boot camp was navy beans for breakfast.

The following Monday morning two hundred and seventy men, us new recruits were transported to an out laying naval air base. Corry field was to be my assignment for the next four years. For me that is, as most of the other men were transferred to a ship in about two years.

Why would I stay four years at the same airbase? I must go back to where we were assembled in a large parking lot, adjacent to a long low building. We were standing at attention and the Chief Petty Officer addressing us asks if there were any volunteers for an electronics job. My hand shot up into the air like it was rocket propelled. The chief noted that I had put my hand up first. (All Chief Petty Officers are addressed as chief, except if you know their last name it can be added to the "chief". I loved being a chief petty officer in the navy but that is another story.)

The chief told me to come see him when we were dismissed. Once again I moved like a rocket, I did not want to miss out on an assignment in electronics. What he said next, liked to floored me. Go inside this building and tell them you have been assigned to the link shack. Link shack, now what in the heck is a link shack? I had no idea, I had never heard of a link shack before.

Going inside was sorta disconcerting because this is a brand new game to me. Once inside I walked up to the receptionist desk and repeated what the chief outside had instructed me to say. I am assigned to the link shack I blunder out. The smile on the young lady's face would have lite up the whole wide world. With that wonderful smile she told me to follow her. The director's office is where she took me. Another Chief, this one didn't smile but directed me to sit in the chair beside his desk.

To make a very long story short I was told of what was expected of me. When I was to report to work, what kind of uniform to wear and a whole lot more things that went right over my head. He talked fast and I tried to listen fast. He closed with you'll catch on in a few days. With a faint smile at my puzzled look, I was told to report to someone, I have no idea who it was. That someone would come get me in a few minutes.

For the next thirty days I was assigned to the clean up crew. Mop this, sweep that or paint it. I soon grew weary of navy gray paint. If it didn't move paint it gray.

When the thirty days were up, boy was I glad to get away from all that painting, I and several other young men were told we would began learning to fly the link trainers. The simulators were designed and build by Ed Link.

The simulators real function was to teach young flight officers how to fly an airplane on instruments. My first job was to learn how to fly a simulator. My dreams have come true. I will learn how to fly on instruments and then I will be instructed on how to teach the actual pilots.

There are several different levels of instrument flying and I was to become a primary teacher. This required I become very proficient at instrument flying. This period of time depended upon ones learning skills. I advanced at a quicker pace than most and I was soon off to the main base, Pensacola Naval Station. This course lasted forty five days. It took every one of those days to learn all the skills necessary to be good at teaching young naval cadets.

I logged over thirty eight hundred hours teaching. Each simulator instructor was provided with a flight log book and each training session was logged with the amount of time and the name of each student. Each entry required the lesson number and how the student pilot was graded.

While working in the link shack I decided this was the field that I wanted to work in. I was an airman apprentice when I arrived at Corry field. I had to wait three months before I could apply for the next level.

Then I am an airman. A step up in rank and a small increase in pay. When I arrived at Corry Field I was paid sixty eight dollars a month. I do not remember my pay going up on achieving the airman rating. A small amount as I remember.

After six months as an airman I took the third class petty officers test. Did not pass the first time. Reason? I didn't study! There was a handbook that the test was taken from. I thought I would learn enough on the job training to pass the test. Just as I had done all through high school. I studied for the next test and passed the test with flying colors.

When my four years was completed I had passed the second class petty officers test but decided to get out of the navy before it became effective.

I was out of the navy a little more than three years. Jobs were hard to find and I decided to go back into the navy and make a career of it.

Arriving at Naval Air station located on the Norfolk Naval Station. I was assigned to the Anti Submarine Warfare division. It was around flying but not directly. I was assigned to a department which taught naval flight crews how to track and kill an enemy submarine. The two techniques I taught were classified as top secret. I would imagine that even the code names are classified now as they were then.

My division officer asked that I teach an extra class on underwater sound to both the pilots and the enlisted flight crews. It was taught once every month and was two hours in length.

I had never been on a ship as a sailor. Yet I was asked to go aboard an aircraft carrier to demonstrate a simulator a chief petty officer and I had developed. The secretary of the navy arrived; I demonstrated the machine and was off the ship in forty five minutes. He could have cared less about having a second class petty office demonstrate a device to allow flight crews to practice anti submarine warfare without having to have a real submarine to track.

I made first class petty officer in the minimum amount of time. I had a desire to make every rating as soon as possible and I did.

While at the Norfolk Naval Station, I put in a request to be sent to the Naval Station where I wanted to attend "B" school for advanced training in my field. The rating I was working in is known as Tradevman or TD. I wanted to go through the advanced level of training for a TD. What I got was a transfer to the TD school staff. As a staff member, not as a student.

What happened? I was assigned to the basic course known as the "A" school as an instructor. I taught through every phase of the "A" school. Never spending more than, a month in each phase. When I had taught all the way through "A" school I was assigned to the advanced level school, known as "B" school. I taught through the first two phases and what was next? Television operation and repair! I liked the phase and was very good at getting the complex subject across to the students.

I was in the television phase for over two years. Two instructors are assigned to each phase so each of us did not have to spend eight hours a day teaching. I had two good partners, in which they carried their share of the teaching load.

For the last year there I had Senior Chief Petty Officers assigned to work with me in the Television phase. Guess what, I taught many eight hour days. The senior chiefs always had something else that required their attention. I was an E6 level rating and the senior chiefs were an E8 level. Being the junior person I was not consulted as to when they would be gone. Many times when my session was up, I would go to our office and no one would be there. So I had to go back and continue with the next lesson.

I enjoyed teaching at the advanced level and I learned a lot having taught through the "A" and "B" levels. I knew there was an assignment coming up that was at a Closed Circuit Television Station and it required an E7 to fill the billet.

I used some influence with one of my teaching partners and finagled the assignment at Naval Mine Warfare School at the Charleston Naval

Station. No flying in this assignment and I will write about that assignment later.

Shortly after arriving at the Naval Mine I received notification that I had been selected for advancement to an E7 level, a chief petty officer.

I sure was happy to receive that news. It sure paid off having taught through both the "A" and "B" schools. Took almost four years but I certainly learned a tremendous lesson. Be careful how you word your requests.

Since I was advanced to the E7 level the navy's policy is and was, to transfer the person to a new duty assignment. I received orders to the Naval Air Station Lemoore. The simulator department at Lemoore had the latest and greatest flight simulators. There were no E7 level billets available so I was assigned to Aviation Physiology Department, while there, a decision made by the leading chief (the petty officer in charge) and he decided where I would find a permanent assignment.

The Av Phy department gave me an opportunity to learn about high altitude low pressure chambers. Pilots and aircrew men were taken to an extremely high altitude in the simulator. Also I was in charge of the pilot's ejection seat trainers.

All were interesting and I enjoyed the experience of each device. However the front office decided that I would start training to replace an E8 Chief Petty Officer. He had received orders upon making the E8 level and was being reassigned per the standard navy procedure upon being advanced to the higher petty officer level.

I must interject here that the "E7, 8, 9 level is considered middle level management.

There were several civilian personnel working at simulator department teaching the advanced level of skills needed for a low level attack aircraft pilot. The most advanced levels being taught to naval aviation pilots.

One of the civilians had a civilian instructor's license and had taught several of the naval personnel assigned to the simulator department. It was at this time I decided to get a private pilot's license.

This story will be told in part two of "Flying"

FLYING
PART II

I sought out the flight instructor and started a conversation. Bob I would like to take flying lessons. How do I get started?

This was the door opener that was needed. Bob explained that there was a small crop duster field about five miles from the air base. There is a small FBO operator stationed on the crop duster field. The operator will rent out his Cessna 150 for eight dollars an hour. If I cared to pay for ten hour blocks it would be five dollars an hour. I quickly told Bob that I wanted to take advantage of the lower price.

Bob told me that he normally charged eight dollars an hour for flight instruction. However since I worked with him and also a sailor with limited income he would charge me five dollars an hour. Wonders of wonders, all these years of wanting to get a license I was getting a good price for the instructor and the airplane. My dream of wanting to fly was finally coming true.

We made arrangements to meet the following afternoon right after his shift ended. He would drive us out to the crop duster field so I would know where to go. Rushing home I excitedly told my wife of my plans. We finally could afford the extra money required. She was none too happy about it but told me to go ahead if that is really what I wanted to do.

The next day I could hardly wait until three thirty P.M. the time Bob's shift ended. I was ready, boy I was really ready. The clock slowly worked its way to the appointed time. I would wear my Chief's uniform for the first lesson. I didn't want to waste an extra minute.

We departed the Naval Base and were soon at the REALLY small strip. The landing area wasn't much over fifteen hundred feet long. AND it had electric power lines and poles on the north end. The power line ran parallel to the roadway we had come in on.

Bob parked right beside the Cessna 150 we would be using. The Cessna is the smallest of the Cessna line of aircraft. It had two seats that looked like it was only large enough for one person. My first lesson started with the pre-flight walk around. Bob explained that every flight HAD to begin with a careful inspection. Once that was completed I got into the left seat and Bob in the right one.

Close but still it allowed for movement for each of us. Next Bob explained every instrument and knob on the instrument panel. I was familiar with most, as the simulators I was proficient in, had the same flight instruments. Finally it came time to start the engine with Bob telling me every step to make. The engine started easily and the propeller turned at a slow rate.

Bob had explained where the brakes were located. Actually there is a brake petal for each wheel. My feet were on the rudder petals and the brakes are on the top of the rudder petals. At first it required much concentration to keep the airplane going in the direction I wanted to go.

We taxied out on to the landing strip as there was no road allowing one to stay off the runway. Both directions were searched for any airplane that might be approaching to land. None were observed and we moved slowly toward the end of the landing strip.

Once at the end Bob directed me as to how to swing the aircraft and have it facing the proper direction for takeoff. Now we did what is called a pre-takeoff check. This involved bring the engine speed up to eighteen hundred RPM. The ignition switch was setting on the BOTH position. Bob directed me to switch to the left magneto and notice the RPM drop. Then the switch is turned back to the both position. Now the switch is turned to the right magneto and once again the RPM is noted.

Each cylinder has two sets of sparkplugs. Each magneto fires a different set of sparkplugs. When the ignition switch is set to the both position both sets of sparkplugs fire and produces a better combustion, therefore a smoother and better running engine.

So far Bob has not touched any of the controls. Now he tells me to bring the engine up to full speed. I'm still holding the brakes on and we have not started to move. Bob's next words were to release brakes and take off. Remember I had trouble taxiing. With the engine running at full speed it is difficult to keep the airplane headed in the direction I wanted it to go. It seemed like I was swinging back and forth a lot. I glanced at Bob and he was sitting relaxed. Finally we reached sixty miles per hour and suddenly the airplane wanted to fly on its own.

Striving to keep the airspeed at sixty miles per hour we were climbing at a brisk five hundred per minute. This is how Bob had described the climb out. Finally he indicated that I was to turn to the right as we were departing the airport flight pattern zone. Bob was using hand movements to indicate what direction I was to fly. Soon we were at three thousand feet and Bob had me to reduce the engine RPM to twenty four hundred RPM.

First I had to learn to fly without depending on the instruments in the cockpit. That's all I had ever used in the flight simulators. It was sorta difficult not to keep my head in cockpit. We practiced making level turns, we practiced climbs and glides. Pretty soon I managed to stay within one hundred feet of the altitude I wanted.

The hour flew by faster than I was flying. It was time to head back to the crop duster field. Bob talked me through the approach and landing. The landing was sorta like a crow hopping about on the ground. A little rough but I managed to not bounce more than three or four times.

My first lesson was on a Tuesday evening and Bob said we would fly again the following Thursday. I could hardly wait. Rushing home I was filled with excitement as I relived my first lesson, then explaining every thing that had happened to my wife and children. I had actually taken off and landed in my very first lesson. This was going to be a piece of cake, I thought. How wrong a person can be, the answer will be answered during the next lesson.

Thursday evening came but this time I went home first and changed into civilian clothing. Now I could be more relaxed in the plane. Bob arrived and we went through the pre-flight just as we had done on the first visit. Everything checked fine and soon we were once again sitting in the airplane at the takeoff end of the run way.

I sat expecting directions from Bob but he just sat there and waited on me to realize that he is not going to say a word. Rather he is causing me to relive the first experience, and do the pre-takeoff check list from memory. Finally I said I was ready to takeoff, he nodded his agreement and said lets go. Once again I struggled to keep the airplane headed down the center of the runway. At sixty miles per hour I applied slight back pressure, to the control wheel and we were airborne. It was much better, than the first takeoff.

This time Bob told me to level off at three hundred feet. We were going to follow some fence rows. Then we made "S" turns across a road. All was done at three hundred feet altitude. I had never flown this low in a simulator. There ain't no ground in a simulator.

After a half hour of flying low Bob directed that I climb to fifteen hundred feet. We were going to practice stalls. First to be done, with no power from the engine. Boy I was amazed as Bob demonstrated a power off stall. First the power is reduced to an idle setting, and then back pressure is applied to the control wheel. The airplane climbs steeply until it loses lift at a slow airspeed of just above thirty miles per hour. The nose of the aircraft drops quickly and the back pressure on the control wheel is released to allow the aircraft to regain flying speed.

Bob tells me I have the controls and tells me to do a no power stall. One is really busy as the airspeed drops off and suddenly the nose of the aircraft is almost pointed at the ground.

We did several more power off stalls when Bob say to do a stall with normal power setting on the engine. It is pretty much like the power off stall except the aircraft wants to turn to the left just as the stall is achieved. Still it is not a normal flight attitude and it will take much practice to feel comfortable.

Next is the full power on stalls. This is to simulate entering a stall while taking off at an airport. This time the airplane really wants to turn left just the stall begins. Lots of right rudder is required and also right aileron is required in order to keep the wings level.

I now had a little over four hours of flight instructions. On our way to the crop duster field Bob said he wanted to do some touch and goes at the Hanford airport. Wow that runway would make three like the one the crop dusters used. It was so big, and so wide! Soon our time was just about up and we headed back to our home base, the crop duster field. Another lesson complete and I was starting to feel a bit more comfortable while flying the airplane.

On our next lesson Bob said we would stay at the crop duster field and practice take off and landings. Little did I know what that would entail or what would happen next? I will never forget that day. We had made three or four take offs and landing. After they were complete Bob said to taxi back to the hanger. As we moved slowly along, taxiing is always done at a very slow speed. Bob said to stop the airplane. Where he promptly opened his door and told me to go back out and make two touch and goes then do a full stop and park the airplane.

With a look of astonishment I asked him did he mean for me to go solo. Was I ready? Could I get the airplane back on the ground safely with out him in the airplane? It finally sunk in that I was to do my first solo flight today. I had done several touch and goes with him in the airplane already. Why should I doubt his judgment now? Well I did doubt myself! I had noticed that Bob had sat through all the touch and goes without saying or doing anything at all.

Surely I could do it!!!!!

I taxied out to the end of the runway and did the usual pre-takeoff check list. The movement of truth had arrived. That great specter of fear crawled slowly up my back. Pushing the throttle full in I prepare to keep the airplane straight as I accelerated down the run way.

Sixty miles per hour and I applied back pressure to the control wheel, climbing out straight ahead until reaching four hundred feet. A gentle left turn and I am doing the cross wind leg of the pattern. Upon reaching eight hundred feet I make a gentle turn to the left for the down wind leg. When even with the end of the runway I reduced the power to idle setting. Starting another left turn to intercept the extended center line of the run way.

Once again I start another turn to the left. Boy, I sure am high to be this close to the runway. Applying full power I prepare to do the approach all over again. This time I would make sure to go a little farther on the down wind leg. Arriving even with the end of the runway I continued for a few seconds more before starting the left hand turn.

Aw, this is more like it. I am out far enough to allow a gentle glide toward the approach end of the runway. Now I am only a few feet above the runway, I start the landing flare, slightly high but I was more secure as the airplane settled toward the landing surface. Bang I hit the runway and crow hopped a few times, but I am safely on the ground.

Pushing the throttle forward I am ready for my second takeoff. Once again I resolved that I would make the down wind leg a little longer to give me more time to get settled into a long glide. Going a bit farther I extended the down wind leg a bit more. This is even better than the last approach. Not as much crow hopping as the airplane settled gently onto the runway surface.

Going around the pattern this time is even better. I feel better. I have more faith in my self to land the airplane safely. Oh yes this will be a full stop and taxi back and park the airplane. Moving slowly on the taxi back I was grinning from ear to ear. As I approached Bob he had a big grin as well.

Moving the airplane to the tie down area I shut the engine down, exited the airplane and locked it. Bob motioned me to follow him to the hanger office. Get your log book too! Running to my car I grabbed my log book and headed into the office. Bob already had his knife out and a blade opened. He congratulated me on my first solo. Next I felt Bob pull my shirt tail out and proceeded to cut a large chunk right in the middle of the shirt it must have been twelve inches wide and about eighteen inches long. He was proudly holding the separated piece of my shirt.

Bob started to write on the cloth, "Fred Sowders first solo", second line was the date and at the bottom he wrote his name. Was I ever proud or what? YES I was! It is a day that I will always cherish. I could hardly wait to get home and tell my wife and family.

Wait a minute, there is the matter of my log book. Remember I only had four hours and a few minutes. Bob took the log book and made two entries, which indicated that I had over six hours of instruction before soloing for the first time.

Then he made an entry indicating I had soloed that day. It is almost impossibility for some one to solo with only four plus hours, which is why Bob fudged the log book to show that my solo occurred during my seventh hour of flight instruction. Arriving home I proudly showed my shirt tail to my family and wife.

Next would come cross country flying. The trip must be to two airports and then return to the small crop duster strip. I never knew when Bob was going to call for a stall. One time we were returning from a cross country flight flying under an overcast sky when he asked for a power on stall. Now we were at about fifteen hundred feet altitude just below the clouds. Always before we would do stalls at three thousand feet.

I pulled back on the control wheel and we were just about to enter the clouds when the stall occurred. The stall was achieved, but we were barely legal. A non instrument rated pilot is never to enter a cloud. Period! I presume that Bob was testing me to see if I would fly into the clouds or not.

After doing the dual cross country flight I was cleared to make my first solo cross country flight. I had done all the planning, knew what navigational aids to use. The flight went uneventful except at every stop I had to add oil to the engine. It was getting tired and burned a lot of oil.

The rest of my training required that I have a total of forty hours of dual and solo flight time. That time soon arrived and I was off to take a flight with a certificated flight instructor.

The oral part of the test went without a hitch. This is due to my extensive experience in the navy and a lot of study at home. There is a written test required by the FAA. I had traveled to Fresno and decided that I would take the commercial written test as well. I passed both tests with a ninety six on one and a ninety eight on the other. I can't remember which score went with what test.

Later in my flight experience I had studied for the instrument rating test and decided that I would take the instrument flight instructor test also. On these two tests I made a ninety two on one and a ninety four on the other. I would have to search through the records one of those days to determine what score went with each test.

I was very proud of the fact that I had scored so well on all of the tests.

On the same day I took the instrument and instrument flight tests, I took the ground instructor test as well as the instrument ground instructor's tests. Passed both but don't remember what the scores were for them.

FLYING
PART III

On the day I passed my private pilot flight test I stopped at the Hanford airport. Going into the FBO office I signed up to start my commercial pilot training. In fact the next day I showed up at the Hanford Flight Training School. I was assigned a flight instructor and had my first commercial hour of training. The Hanford Flight Training school used a low wing Piper PA 23 aircraft. It is much larger than a Cessna 150. It had seating for four. A hundred and fifty horse power engine. Where as the Cessna 150 has a hundred horse-power engine. A new experience, one I thoroughly enjoyed. The Piper PA 23 cruised at one hundred thirty miles per hour; where as the Cessna 150 cruised at one hundred miles per hour.

I had a very young man as my instructor who was building flight hours so he could apply to one of the major airlines for a job. A pilot had to have two thousand hours to even be considered. Their cut off age was thirty five years old. Oh well I could never be an Air Transport Pilot (ATP, as it is commonly called) as I am over forty.

I can't even recall the young man's name. But I must say I had to have a bunch of hours, two hundred to be specific. I had forty hours after the private pilot's test, so I needed one hundred sixty hours for the commercial pilots test. We followed roads at a very low level. We followed rivers, again at a very low level. We tried out small out of the way airports. One he chose was grown up with weeds. Actually the airport was closed but it was still available for any pilot that had the guts to try landing in a field of tall weeds. When we got back to the Hanford airport we had to clean a lot of weeds out of the landing gear.

One time my oldest daughter wanted to visit a college in the bay area. How to get there? We flew up, took a taxi to the college. I had never been to the airport and it was a very busy airfield, Livermore. I asked my instructor to go along and call it a cross country training flight.

We did have to land at another airport for it to be a legal cross country flight. We did and now I can't even remember where the airport was located. I would have to go back into my flight logs to see what the name was.

I received transfer orders to the Mare Island Naval base about this time. I flew to a near by airport at the town of Vacaville and got a tour of the naval base. I inquired about a flight club at the Travis Air Force Base. They had one and I hurried to the Air Force Base and soon located the flight club. I immediately applied for membership and was accepted as a commercial pilot trainee. I only needed about twenty more hours to be qualified for the flight test. As I had already passed the written test there was no need to study for another test.

I was assigned to a retired air force pilot as my instructor. The club had both high and low wing aircraft. I was already checked out in all of the types of aircraft that were available for flight instruction.

My duty assignment was in a training devices division. The E-8 in charge of the division had worked for me when we were stationed at Norfolk. He was very lenient about my aspirations of becoming a commercial pilot. I could have as much time off as the flight schedule at the club allowed. I flew three times a week as I could be available during the normal working hours. Most of the students had to schedule their flights after they had completed a day's work. I was very fortunate.

I garnered all the necessary dual and solo flight time needed for the commercial flight test. Passed it with flying colors, so to speak. Really it was a piece of cake. I had no problems at all, doing the required maneuvers.

One thing I left out of the training at Hanford. When I was working on the private pilot license, I wanted to learn how to enter a spin and then recover from the spin. Bob and I flew to a small airport south of Fresno, California, where I rented a small Cessna 150 that was certified for spins.

Bob did the first spin and scared the crap out of me. Just as the aircraft stalled he kicked in full left rudder. The airplane rolled to the left and Bob gave out a blood curding scream. I was really not sure of what was happening until I looked at him and he had the biggest smile I had ever seen. Then I knew that we were not in any danger, such as falling out of the sky.

I climbed the airplane back up to five thousand feet and did a spin to the left just as Bob had done. We also spun the airplane to the right.

In my log book he made an entry for spins left and right with his signature.

Also while at Hanford I asked my young flight if we could spend an hour practicing spins. The FBO (fixed base operator) had only one aircraft certified for spins. We checked and the plane was not scheduled that afternoon. Off we went to practice spins. I already had a log book entry that I was checked out in spins left and right but wanted to practice so I would be comfortable during the whole spin.

Once again I leveled the airplane at five thousand feet. I made clearing turns to the left and to the right. Making sure there were no other aircraft in the area I was going to spin the airplane. Power off I pulled the nose up to a thirty-degree angle. The airspeed bleeds off quickly. Just as the airplane began to enter a stall I pulled the control wheel completely back and kicked in full left rudder. Boy did that Cessna 170 spin fast, much faster than the Cessna 150 I had flown before.

We did three fast revolutions and made a normal recovery. Not bad I thought. Several more spins were done, both to the left and to the right. The airplane spun slightly slower going to the right. I was feeling comfortable and started to climb for a seventh spin when my instructor said lets quit, my stomach is getting upset. With that we headed back to the airport.

Now back to flying at the Travis Air Force base. I had just completed the commercial pilot's flight test. I signed up to work on an Instructors rating. The entire course required that I fly the aircraft from the right seat of the airplane. This meant that I had to re-qualify in all of the airplanes available at the flight club.

The course also required that I fly from the right seat and teach all of the maneuvers I had already learned. Still I had to demonstrate to the schools Chief Flight Instructor that I was competent to do everything from the right seat. It didn't take any time at all to adjust to flying from the right seat. It merely was switching the function of both hands.

I now have completed all the required flight instruction. I went to the FFA office in Sacramento, California. All flight instructors have to teach an already qualified pilot and be very, very critical of very move they made. In fact I was super critical of even the smallest of control moments. That's what the inspector is looking for. Once again I passed with flying colors.

When the flight test was over I walked out as a Certified Flight Instructor. I had less than two hundred and fifty hours total time.

Now to get some students lined up and began a new phase of flying. My first student will be introduced in "Flying part IV"

Flying
Part IV

I am now a full-fledged flight instructor and ready to take on the task of teaching others to do, what I love to do, flying. For some time a friend at our church and I had been talking flying. Any time some one wanted to talk flying I was always ready.

Denton and I had had many such talks. He had taken four or five lessons several years ago. I told him in all likely-hood he would have to start over with his flying lessons.

What I must interject at this point is the fact that Denton had had polio as a child. The left side of his body had been affected. He walked with a limp and sorta dragged his left foot. How much use he had of the left foot and leg would be determined in the airplane. When driving he had to manually lift the left foot to the brake pedal.

I had told Denton about how close I was to getting my teaching Certificate. We made plans and he would be my first student. What we needed now was to be able to rent an airplane.

I drove to the Napa airport and checked with the chief flight instructor. I told Brig of receiving my teaching certificate and my plans for my first student. I asked if it would be possible to rent an aircraft from his flight service company! He said that I would have to take a flight with him to ensure that I could fly the airplane and could do all of the maneuvers that the private pilot would have to perform.

Soon we were on our way out to the flight line and located the airplane we were to use. I did a very detailed preflight inspection of the aircraft. When that was finished I walked to the right side of the aircraft and got in the airplane.

Brig is a rather large individual and he had to squeeze in but did manage to get his door shut. I did my normal checklist and we were soon in the air. Brig asked that I level at five hundred feet and proceed out of the airport traffic area. He pointed out a roadway and asked that I do "S" turns across it. To make a long story shorter I demonstrated every maneuver that was on the commercial flight test.

After more than fifty minutes Brig said lets go back to the airport, you can use aircraft any time you want. That would good news for Denton as well

After parking and tying down the airplane we walked back into the office. I pulled out my wallet in anticipation of paying for the check ride Brig smiled and say "this is on the company, there is no charge. Wow and double wow that was right decent of him and the company. I scheduled an airplane for the following Thursday evening for Denton's first lesson.

Upon arriving back home I called Denton and told him the good news. He was ecstatic and I cannot describe the happiness that was in his voice. He said he could hardly wait until Thursday evening to get here.

Denton came to my house Thursday just as soon as he got off from work and we were off to the airport. It is only about six to ten minutes and we were there in no time.

Getting out of the car we go in to the Bridgeford Flying Service office. Brig once again greeted me and I introduced Denton. Brig showed no facial change when he saw Denton. The average person would wonder if Denton could get into the airplane much less fly it.

What Brig did do was to ask me to come see him when we landed; he had something he wanted to discuss in private.

I did the walk around preflight inspection and explained to Denton the importance of checking everything on the airplane before even considering flying it.

Preflight done we get into the airplane and I went over every instrument, knob, and control explaining the function of each. This alone took more than twenty minutes, long but worth every second spent on doing the proper introduction to Denton.

Now it is time to start the engine and start taxiing to the takeoff run way. I demonstrated each action and then let Denton continue. We pulled into the engine run up area and did all the usual checks. Denton was a quick learner and soon we were ready for the takeoff.

On my first attempt at taking off my instructor sat there and let me do it all. I did the same with Denton, we were all over the runway, but we made a safe takeoff. Some would ask how can you sit there and let a novice take off. My reply was my hands and feet are never far from the controls. Always close enough to help if the help is needed. In all of my teaching I have had to take the controls only one time.

A woman I was working with was almost ready to solo. We had been doing take offs and landings for thirty minutes. I had not had to say one word to her about her flying during the whole time. We were just about to touch down when she suddenly shoved the control wheel all the way forward. I had to react really quickly or the nose wheel would have hit the runway very, very hard. Fortunely I was quick enough that there was no damage to the engine firewall where the front landing gear is attached.

When Denton and I had finished all the paper work and was ready to leave the building I found Brig and asked what he wanted to talk to me about. Well I must tell you that I just about jumped out of my shin when he asked me to join his staff and teach full or part time, whatever I wanted to do.

Pleasure of pleasures, joy of joys I had just been offered a job teaching flying. How much better can it get? It was a dream, come true. Of course I accepted his offer and told him I would be pleased to join his staff.

In no time at all I had more students than I could handle on a part time basis but that is another story and will be told in another episode of flying.

Denton was about average in learning all of the maneuvers necessary to earn a private pilots license. Some he learned quickly and some it took a little longer to accomplish a task.

We were about three hours of flight time short of the necessary forty hours needed. We were practicing stalls which Denton had done many times before. Actually what I was doing was actually having him do every thing that the examiner would ask him to do.

We were just entering the beginning of a power off stall when Denton stopped working the controls to effect a recover. Why he froze I have no idea, I asked him later, and he did not have an answer. So we did many stalls after that and he did them perfectly each time. Maybe his brain got tired and took him somewhere else!

Just before Denton was to take his check ride Brig came to me and said that he had some doubts about Denton's ability to control the aircraft with his bad left leg. I told Brig that I was comfortable recommending Denton for the check ride but if at the conclusion that he still had doubts then by all means send him to the FAA for a ride with one of their check pilots.

When Denton and Brig walked back into the office after the check ride Denton had the biggest smile on his face. I knew at the moment that he had done a good job and demonstrated his ability to fly the airplane.

Later I talked to Brig and he was very pleased with the check ride. I asked if it was ok to check Denton out in a Cessna 172 which is a four-place airplane. With no hesitation Brig said he had no reason to deny him the opportunity to be checked out in the aircraft.

It was a pleasure to check Denton out in the Cessna 172. One hour and I signed him off "safe to solo a C-172.

To my knowledge Denton never took him family flying, in fact I do not think he ever got in an airplane again. He accomplished what he wanted to do. He did earn his private pilots license. What more did he have to prove?

FLYING
PART V

I enjoyed instructing each day. I am still in love with flying. I am doing it six days a week now. I refused to work Sundays. At least I had one day that was not devoted to flying. I still had the love of getting in an airplane and being free to go where ever one wanted to go. We flew a lot, my wife and me, and took many people with us. We would fly to an airport that had a restaurant on the field or close by where we could walk to it.

One day I was in my office doing paper work that never seemed to be done. It was an endless toil because much paper work had to be submitted each month. There was a knock on the door and a man walked in and inquired if he could get a flight instructor rating at our school. Bill had retired from the air force as a full colonel. He had been in the air force thirty years. Now he wanted to take a job that required he have a flight instructors license.

Being the oldest pilot on the staff I suggest to Bill that I work with him on achieving his goal. At that time the FAA required that all students do their training in a retractable wheel aircraft and that it is classified as a complex airplane.

We only had one aircraft that met the requirements a Cessna 200. It had a two hundred horse power engine, which was a requirement. It was a retractable landing gear airplane. Bill and I had the job of helping him to learn to fly light aircraft. All his flying had been done in the air force. He was a fighter pilot with several trips to Vietnam. He had many interesting stories of his experiences.

The course required twenty hours of flight instruction and twenty hours of ground instruction. It didn't require much that Bill had to learn. I would simply take him out and let him learn how to fly a light aircraft. We had many hours to simply play, if you will. He could fly as well as me. Maybe better!

It kept me on my toes to stay ahead of the game. I devised many unusual flight activities for him. One day I told Bill we were going to climb out over the Chesapeake Bay and do lazy eights at five thousand feet. It was no time at all until Bill has mastered the lazy eight maneuvers. What he didn't know was the fact that I had contacted the Napa airport tower and told them we would like to do simulated engine out procedure beginning at five thousand feet.

Heading back to the airport I asked Bill to keep the altitude at five thousand feet. He gave me an inquiring look but I did not response to his inquisitive look. When we were directly over the airport I told Bill I had control of the airplane. Since I am in the right seat I reached up with my left hand and pulled the gasoline mixture control back to cutoff. In other words the engine quits running. The propeller was still being turned by the on coming air at a hundred forty miles per hour.

I applied gentle back pressure on the control wheel and the airspeed bleed off quickly. The propeller stopped turning. Now we are a full time glider. Smiling I told Bill that he once again had control of the airplane. I told him that since we were directly over the airport that we would glide down in a steep banked turn. Keeping the left wing tip pointed directly at the approach end of the run way.

I called the tower controller and told him that we had entered a simulated engine our procedure at five thousand feet directly above the airport. The controller acknowledged our request and to report when we turned down wind. Continuing our descent we passed over the runway at fifteen hundred feet and I told Bill to turn down wind and I reported the down wind turn to the tower.

Having an engine running and having the power available is one thing. But to not have any power available at all is quite another situation. Bill wanted to turn cross wind too soon and was still too high to make a landing at or near the numbers painted on the approach end of the runway.

I asked him to extend the down wind leg a bit more before turning on the base leg. Now we were just about right in my opinion to turn and I told Bill to commence the base leg turn.

Now he was on his own as to when to put the flaps down and to flair for the landing. We touched down about seventy five feet beyond the numbers. Not bad for his first ever, real engine out landing. It was something that he had never done before. Bill was pleased and so was I.

We did many more overhead approaches. It all ways done with the engine off, and the prop not moving.

I have always wondered what the tower controller thought when we came in on short final and he could see that the propeller was not turning. They never called and I never asked.

There is something I would like to add at the end of this story. I loved flying so much that I would take a short flight after the days training was over. I would take a Cessna 150 out for two touch and go's. Doing the engine run up and test, while taxiing toward the take off end of the runway. Normally this would all be done after arriving at the departure end of the runway, in an area called the run up area. I saved a lot of time by doing all the checks as I approached the end of the run way.

I would ask the tower controller to make two touch and go's and a full stop landing. The airport traffic was always light at this time of the day. So there was not traffic to contend with. After receiving clearance for take off, full power would be applied. Since I am the only one in the airplane it accelerates quickly and climbs rapidly. As I approach the landing end of the runway power is reduced to idle speed. I would push in almost full right rudder and at the same time start a left hand bank. This would put the airplane almost flying on the side of the fuselage instead of the wings. This procedure was taught before flaps were added to all the aircraft. Still I wanted to learn the procedure and be proficient as much as possible.

One day a tower controller did call and ask where I had learned to slip the aircraft like I was doing. I merely replied that I was self taught.

FLYING
PART VI

A little more than a year has passed since I become a part time flight instructor for Bridgeford Flying Service FBO. The school has a full time chief flight instructor. It also has a full time director of operations. The man, who is presently the Director of Operations, decided that he wanted to quit and go full time writing books. It was the talk of the office and among all of the flight instructors.

One of the owners of the FBO asked me to his office for a meeting. I had no idea what it concerned. Jack asked to close the door and have a seat. Once again I didn't have a clue of what he wanted to discuss. Jack asks that I take the job of Director of Flight School position. My mind was spinning! I am still on active duty in the navy. I would have to retire soon. I told Jack that I needed a few days before I made a decision. With that I completed the flight hours I had scheduled and headed home to discuss the situation with my wife. All of our children were now married and living on their own.

Yes I wanted to take the position! No I was not ready to retire from the navy. The navy had been good to me, and for me. The next day I talked to the officer in charge of my division. He didn't help me any at all. Next I went to the personnel office to see if I could put my papers in to retire. How much time would it take? I still had many questions to answer in my mind. To make a long story short I did decide to retire and take the position with Bridgeford Flying Service. Once the decision had been made I felt a sense of relief. It was as if a large weight had been taken off my shoulders.

I was set to retire September 30, 1975. The time passed quickly and all told it took three weeks to be processed out of the navy and onto the Navy Retired list. I retired one day and the next I started working full time for Bridgeford Flying Service. I had my own office and a lot of paperwork to do. All of the paper work the FAA required for a certified flight school. Then there was the paperwork for those people that were studying under the G.I. bill. There was a ton of correspondence to keep up with.

All this and I kept all my flight students. I tried to fly at least four hours a day. Most do no realize that for each hour flown it requires two hours on the ground. I tried to keep the ground time to minimum as much as possible. I got it down to about one hour on the ground for each hour in the air.

This continued until March 1978, I woke up one Sunday morning early. To make a long story short I suffered a heart attack and had heart by-pass heart surgery. My flying career had come to an abrupt end.

This was a devastating time in my life. My life was turned upside down.

Never to fly again!

FLYING
PART VII

Well time sure flies even when you are not having fun. I had suffered a heart attack with heart by-pass surgery ten days later. It took a long time to recover. I did not know what to expect. I didn't know how I should feel. My former secretary had quit working at Bridgeford Flying Service and taken a job with IASCO, International Air services Co. While there she found out that another simulator tech was needed. She talked with Daryl and he told her he had worked for me when we were stationed at NAS Lemoore.

What a small world it is. Daryl had been with IASCO for a little over a year. Chris and Daryl talked and she told him of my situation. Daryl called and we talked and he invited me out the next day. Little did I know that it was to be a job interview. Upon arriving at the flight training center, Daryl told me that IASCO was a management company and they had a contract with Japan Airlines to provide all the flight instructors and other maintenance personnel for teaching the Japanese students to fly.

Napa airport is where all of the JAL airline student pilots are taught. They start here because it is cheaper than in Japan. There is more airspace for them to use. Last it is an English speaking environment.

Those three factors caused the beginning students to be taught to fly at the Napa airport.

Daryl was in charge of the flight simulators. He was the only person in the department and he needed help. He needed a qualified simulator technician. There is a full flight simulator with a motion base. Next were two Link trainers and last a twin engine simulator.

The Japanese were increasing their total number of students. We had been told that eventually the number of students at any one time would climb to over two hundred. They presently had forty to fifty students.

The full flight simulator was being scheduled more hours each day. This made for a very long day as Daryl had to come in an hour early before the first scheduled flight of the day. He had to stay and clean up the simulators after the last flight of the day. No wonder he needed help and fast.

As we concluded our conversation Daryl asked me to come to work the following Monday which was the first working day of the year 1980.

I worked for Daryl for ten years. He believed in the chewing gum and rubber band treatment to keep the simulators running. Still I had a good job which required little or no work for me. Daryl would come in an hour before the first scheduled flight and I would come in so that I would be there an hour after the last scheduled flight. I have to post flight the simulators and clean them as necessary. If a simulator broke down it was usually both of us were there.

The years flew by and I was content to do whatever Daryl wished. In 1990 Daryl decided that he wanted to reach out for a higher level of management. He approached the General Manager and made his desires known. In a week or so Daryl was called to the general manager's office and offered the job of assistant manager. He accepted the job on the spot. Next they discussed me as being the manager of the simulator department. When Daryl came back to our little office he said that the GM wanted me to come to his office. He did not give me a hint that he had been advanced or that I was to succeed him.

I should go back and tell that our work load had increased quite a lot. Daryl had me to put a want add in several of the local papers. Don was among those interviewed and was selected for the position. Now I had to go through the screening process once again as we needed three people to carry the work load. The student count was at about one hundred and we had just been told that there would be four hundred and fifty pilots retiring by 1995. This means a huge increase in the student load as it takes two years for the students to complete their training at the Napa facility.

About two months after I had accepted the position of manager of the simulator department my Japanese boss asked me to come to his office for a meeting. Once again I have no idea what to expect. When I sat down and was introduced to the five men present they informed me that JAL was going to buy a simulator. What size room would be needed?

First there are several questions I needed to ask. What size simulator? Would it have six degrees of freedom motion base? I asked all of the questions and they had no answers for each of my questions. They had been told they were buying a simulator. They didn't know what company it would be purchased from.

Off the top of my head I told them I would need a fifty by fifty foot room with a thirty five foot ceiling. I would be safe with that answer. I could put any simulator made today in that size room. A week later I was asked to come to the Japanese boss's office. He wanted me to go to the Flight Safety Simulator Company located in Broken Arrow, Oklahoma. I asked about what I was to do there. He said that I was to tour the factory and take as many photographs as possible. He still did not know what size simulator the company would purchase.

I called the manager of the Flight Safety Company and informed him that I would be arriving two days later. Would he please make arrangements for a hotel and arrange to have me picked up at the airport. He was more than willing but wanted to know what company I represented. What else could I tell him but Japan Airlines had asked me to visit their factory for them and gather as much information as possible.

They did not have a contract to build a simulator for Japan Airline, yet here I am practically telling them that they would be getting a contract soon. I didn't know but it sure didn't hurt giving Flight Safety the impression that JAL would purchase from them. I toured the factory, took hundreds of photographs and asked a thousand questions. From what size motion base would be used to how large a concrete base would be needed.

When I arrived back at Napa my Japanese boss was eager to talk with me and get as many details as possible. Remember that the locals and Flight Safety personnel had no details as to what would be purchased. This was to change quickly. Two days later a gentleman that worked in JAL's purchasing department arrived at Napa. Now maybe there will be some answers.

To my surprise the official from purchasing had deliberately not contacted Flight Safety. But he did want them to know that Flight Safety had been chosen to build the simulator. What a crazy way to conduct business. I could have certainly used the information to leverage a lower price for the simulator. Well I did do just that, but it was at a later meeting. After the Japanese had formally contacted Flight Safety a meeting was arranged for four days later. Guess who was in charge of the whole shebang? Me!

I did all of the formal talking, the Japanese man for purchasing was using me as a go between. Flight Safety wanted fourteen million to build a simulator. They did not have any specs nor did they know what aircraft was to be simulated. They were just setting a high price, knowing they could build the simulator for a lower price. After much haggling I finally got tired of going back and forth. I said to the manager of Flight Safety," we will give you ten million to build the simulator to JAL specs". After much private talking and running back and forth, the manager told me they would accept the offer. Now I had to go to the JAL purchasing agent and convince him that it was a good price quote.

He laughed and said that it was a million less than what he was willing to accept. How about that, I am a negotiator and did not know it. I had just picked a number out of the air and it worked. Don't ask how I came up with that number. I don't know how I arrived at the number. Pure luck, and a lot of knowledge of simulators, nothing else.

The Japanese were happy; Flight Safety was happy, what was left? Well there were a ton of meetings required to spell out every aspect of the job. When would it be started? When would it be completed? What kind of acceptance testing would be needed?

JAL wanted a simulator for the Falcon 20 aircraft. What Flight Safety did not know was the fact that there was no flight data available, which was needed to build the flight profile for the simulator. Once again we were involved in making decisions; JAL would provide the airplane and flight crew for a three week period. Flight Safety was to provide all the testing equipment and personnel to accomplish the task. Testing on the airplane began in early November 1990. I didn't have any responsibilities while this was taking place.

Our next meeting took place in early December where the tentative schedule of construction was accepted by JAL. Meetings at Flight Safety would start in January and be every two weeks or sooner if needed.

What I have not interjected at this point is the fact that JAL wanted a wrap around visual system for the simulator. Flight Safety recommended McDonald Douglas visual system. A meeting was arranged and once again my Japanese counter parts and I flew to St. Louis to visit the plant that would be building the visual system. Did I tell you that I was the only white man representing the Japanese? There was always three or more Japanese.

Flight Safety took all of us out every evening for dinner. They also took us to lunch every day. These were not cheap meals and they always catered to high end restaurants and they strived to ensure that there was always a Japanese restaurant or two planned for every trip.

Now with the visual system in our schedule we were gone just about every week for the next two years with a meeting at either Flight Safety or at the Mc Donald Douglas visual plant at ST Louis, Mo.

Now to go back and pick up some loose ends! Right after returning from the first visit to Flight Safety, I was asked to visit the office of the Japanese man that was in charge of buildings and such other things, as the Director of the flight school wanted.

Kaz wanted to discuss the building of a structure to house the new simulator. I gave him my original numbers to which he did not seemed surprised. What he did, was to surprise me by saying that JAL needed eleven new classrooms. Each room was to be large enough for twenty two students. Also he wanted two English class rooms to handle the same amount of students.

That was not hard to determine as California dictated that each student have twenty two square feet of floor space. Each class room would have a minimum of four hundred eighty four feet. This meant that eleven class rooms would require five thousand three hundred twenty four feet.

Not hard to determine what the total footage needed would be. All I had to do was add the requirements for the English Class rooms. A couple or three rooms for the staffing requirements and I could arrive at the total amount of space needed on the second floor level.

The floor below was designated for four simulators. With two rooms having removable outside walls for the actual movement of the device into the space. I was planning for a staffing level of twelve maintenance techs. Lower level complete! Now to the large simulator with the motion base and visual system and the space it would require.

I knew we would be getting one of the large simulators. I needed to convince the JAL boss that while we were building we should make space for a possible second large device to be added later. There was no argument from him. He agreed that it would be cheaper to build now rather than two to five years later.

Kaz asked that I start drawing up plans for the complete building. He did however want an estimated amount the total building would cost. He had to go to Japan and do whatever was necessary to get the funding.

Mean time I was to proceed with interviewing all of the different companies that would be needed. There was no one better qualified to do this on IASCO's staff. I had just gone through the same things when I had a large garage built at my home. I already knew what the going rate was per square foot for the construction. The special flooring requirements for the motion base were a calculated risk and I planned for two hundred twenty five dollars per square foot.

I came up with a total of six million and eighty five thousand dollars to build the complete structure. Guess what the total turned out to be? A little less than six and a half million dollars. Kaz had guess-ta-mated seven point three million dollars. So we both were high but I was closer than he was.

Kaz made several trips to Japan and did come up with the necessary funding. Glad I was not involved in the negotiations he had to do in order to be granted the funds that we would need. A ten million dollar simulator, six point four million for the building. One million dollars for spare parts to maintain the simulator for a twenty-four hour working day.

I traveled around the countryside interviewing contractors, architects and a host of other companies. Kaz asked me to bring three of my top chooses in for a personal interview with him. However he did make one request, that the one I favored the most would always be last. Guess what happened? He always chose the last one involved in the interviews. It didn't take long for me to catch on to his plan. He didn't want to put in a great deal of time in all of the interviews. He was letting me know that whoever I believed was best would be alright with him.

I did enjoy a lot of prestige and power working for JAL. I am in charge of getting a lot done. However I have not mentioned that I was also involved in the purchasing of airplanes for JAL. I made many trips to the Piper aircraft manufacturing plant for forty plus new airplanes. The airplanes cost a little over twenty two million dollars. I got to tour the factory many times. And I arranged the delivery schedule for all of the aircraft.

Going back to the time I made the first trip to Flight Safety's simulator division. Upon my return I was called to Kaz's office and he wanted me to negotiate with the Napa County Supervisory board to lease land next to the land that was presently leased for the flight school.

Here again there was no one on IASCO's staff that had the necessary experience to do the negations for JAL. I contacted the Napa County Supervisory board and was told to make contact with the Napa County Airport Director. That he would handle all of the agreements for leasing land on the Napa County Airport. I already knew Lenard and called for an appointment to meet with him.

To make a long story short, because there were many trips back and forth between the two offices, but we agreed on a price of two dollars and twenty four cents a square foot for a ninety nine year lease. At the end of the lease period the structures on the land would then be owned by the Napa County Airport Department.

After this contract was signed sealed and delivered, Kaz asks me to lease as much additional land as I could get. Once again to make a long story short I arranged leases for just over nine acres of land for the Japanese.

As you can see during the early years of the nineties I was involved in almost every thing the Japanese did at the Napa county airport. Purchasing airplanes, the construction of a new building, and the purchase of three smaller simulators I have not mentioned. The leasing of land and several other projects, one of which involved the installation of a new twelve inch water line to serve both the airport and JAL's facility. I was also involved in the installation of a new fuel storage site for the airport.

I enjoyed those years, I was very involved and I put in many twelve hour days to get it all done.

There is thousands of additions words I could add but to sum it all up, a new building was build, airplanes were purchased, a new large full flight simulator was built and delivered. Land was leased and the Japanese were happy.

I didn't get an increase in pay for all the work I did. I do know that IASCO increased the fee they charged for me to over one hundred thousand dollars a year. I did not see a penny more than the forty thousand a year I received for several years.

It is a long story and involved a General Manager that I did not get along with. I will not go into the details.

When I first joined the IASCO staff, IASCO charged a standard mark up of twenty five per cent on all salaries, parts purchased for airplanes and all maintenance items. A healthily profit margin. What IASCO would do is purchase everything at wholesale. Charge full retail price to JAL and then add the twenty five per cent to that price.

At one time I tried to get the contract to operate the training facility for JAL. Their answer was "we would rather deal with the snake we know than to take on a new one". Direct and to the point. Little did I know that JAL had plans to get several hundreds of millions of dollars back from IASCO. If they were to grant a new contract they would not be able to recoup that money.

I retired at the end of 1999. The full flight simulator was sold and not replaced. In fact I was told to reduce the simulator staff by two people. There was an incentive, two months pay to be laid off. I chose to be one of the personnel to be laid off. I was ready to retire.

I was fortunate enough to be one of the few people in the world that have been involved in the purchase of a new simulator with a wrap around visual system. At the same time to be involved in the construction of a new training building. At the same time be involved in the leasing of so much land for JAL. Last but not least, the purchasing of so many new airplanes.

How lucky can one person be to do it all at the same time!

CRASH REPORT

12 March 1976

Date: 18 February 1976
Aircraft: Cessna 210 N2230S
Pilot: George Cline
Co-Pilot: Frederick Sowders
Passenger: Senator Laxalt of Nevada
Location: Napa County Airport

Sometime mid-afternoon of February 18, 1976, I checked the schedule board. George, one of Napa County Airport's pilot, was scheduled for a charter flight with a N2060Q a Cessna 177RG to San Francisco. This airplane had developed a hydraulic leak in the landing gear system while on a training flight and had returned at approximately 1730 (5:30 P.M. local time). The charter flight was then changed to a Cessna 182.

George informed me at about 1830 (6:30 P.M. local time), that if the weather continued to get windy and rainy, he would need a co-pilot for the flight. He asked if I would go with him if needed. After we discussed weather, I went home to eat dinner. I called George at 2045 (8:45 P.M. local time) to see if he still needed me. He indicated I was needed. We had company for the evening so I was hesitate in going, but figured the flight wouldn't take long and I could soon be back home.

I arrived at the Napa Airport Bridgeford office at 2105 (9:15 P.M. local time). George had gone to the hanger for the Cessna 210. The flight was scheduled for a party of three but required the use of a six place airplane.

Upon my arrival to the hanger, I helped tow the airplane outside and George taxied it to the front of the terminal building. I walked to the building and talked with two friends as we watched George do a pre-flight line check of the aircraft. Then, George and I reviewed the approach procedures for the San Francisco trip.

The U.S. Senator arrived at approximately 2140 (9:40 P.M. local time). George informed him of the weather conditions and the requirement for an additional pilot. At that time we were informed that there would be only one passenger for the flight.

The Senator was running behind schedule but informed us it was very important he make the 2300 (11:00 P.M. local time) flight from San Francisco to Washington, D.C.

We loaded the Senator and his luggage aboard the aircraft. Upon entering the airplane as the copilot, it was my responsibility to set up the approach procedures and prepare to copy our IFR clearance. By this time we were at the run-up area. George did the pre-takeoff checklist while I copied the clearance and did the read back.

While waiting for the IFR release from the tower we were told there was an aircraft on the instrument approach and there would be a delay.

George told the tower that he was shutting down the engine and would monitor the frequency. George asked the tower if they would get the latest weather report for San Francisco. Approximately 8 to 10 minutes later the tower called and said to start the engine and taxi into position for take-off.

After being cleared by the tower for take off, we proceeded to the Napa VOR (local navigation station) and leveled at 4000 feet MSL. After passing San Pablo intersection we received a radar vector from Bay Approach to turn to a heading directly to the San Francisco Airport. Shortly after, the engine began to run rough. I noticed that George turned the fuel selector from the right tank to the left tank. Later George instructed me to request a lower altitude from the approach control. This was granted and we descended to 3000 feet MSL.

We passed Berkley intersection, and I had set up for the South Shore intersection. (This is a radio fix to determine location) Shortly afterward the engine started running rough again. I asked George what was wrong, and he replied he believed the airplane was out of fuel. I looked up from the approach procedure chart and both fuel gauges indicated empty. The engine stopped running and George instructed me to declare an 'emergency', which I did.

The Controller gave several instructions and told us to turn left 30 degrees for the Oakland Airport and gave the height of the ceiling. Oakland was almost on the nose of the aircraft when we broke out of the overcast at approximately 1300 feet MSL. (Mean Sea Level-which is the Airplane's height about the water.)

I informed the Senator that we were making an emergency landing and instructed him to position himself. I was not sure we would be able to glide to the airport. I asked the controller what was in the area short of the runway. He did not answer or at least I do not remember hearing if he did. We then impacted the water, which was three to four feet deep. I informed the controller that everyone was okay, and that the airplane was setting on the bottom and that we were staying in the aircraft.

Thirty to forty minutes later we were picked up in a basket by a Coast Guard helicopter. We were taken to Vesper Memorial hospital in San Leandro, where we were checked for injuries and released. Luckily there were no injuries, not even a scratch.

The next day I was informed by Bridgeford Personal, that Cessna 210, N2230S, had returned from a charter flight on February 13th from the Los Angles area. The pilot noticed an unsafe gear indicator upon the return to the Napa Airport. He circled to burn off fuel, and then flew by the tower for a visual check. After landing he taxied directly to the maintenance hanger.

This was Friday evening and close to closing time. The pilot wanted to have the aircraft checked before the weekend. The unsafe gear indication was checked, and was found to be a micro switch malfunction.

I did not line check the aircraft, therefore I did not know the amount of fuel aboard the aircraft.

SECTION IV

SPECIAL PEOPLE

GEORGE

When we started racing in 1979 George and Suzie were a part of the crew that took care of the race car. They were what we then called the dirt pickers. Every time the car came off the race track there was mud everywhere and had to be removed. The track was dirt and before the race cars ever entered the race track the track owners would break up the surface and put tons of water on it. The race track had to be packed and work the water into the dirt until there is a good racing surface.

Back to the real beginning, my son Steve owned a 1968 Pontiac. He bought the car in Indiana and brought the car with him when he and his family moved to California. Having been in Indiana and driven on the winter weather roads a lot of the salt had gotten up into the fender panels and caused a lot of rust damage. Steve talked to me about making the car into a race car. He and I had attended the local track to watch the racing. There was a class which was called the "bomber" class. It required the roll bars but the most unusual requirement was that there had to be a passenger in the car as well.

Steve wanted to make his car qualify for the bomber class. My daughter's husband George volunteered to be the shotgun passenger. Now I would not have gotten into a race car if I couldn't be the driver. But George seemed anxious to be a part of the racing team. We set about stripping out the interior of the car. We removed all of the glass windows from the car! Had roll bars installed! Cut off as much of the sheet metal as required. The rules required a twelve-inch hole in the hood over the carburetor, in case there was an engine fire it could be gotten to quickly.

The car was a tan color which was not a suitable for a race car, at least in our eyes. George's brother worked in a paint shop and was persuaded to not only to provide the paint, he would paint the car as well. Why the dark blue color was chosen I have not idea, but we now had a deep blue color race car.

The rules did not allow any changes to the suspension, nor to the tires. Everything had to be as the car ran on the street. What we did not think about was the fact that this car had tubeless tires, as most cars did at that time. The reason will make itself evident latter.

The racing season had already started when we began to make the car into a race car. We did not get it track ready until the end of May.

Although we lived three blocks from the race track not a thought had entered our minds about how we would get the car to the race track. Once again George came to the rescue. He knew a man that had a trailer. He talked him into letting us borrow his trailer.

We made plans for our first race to be the first weekend of June. We arrived at the track early and got the car unloaded. Got a pit spot close to Skip Brown, who lived three houses to the north of my house. Skip had been racing for many years and had given us many helpful hints in the construction of our race car.

The track announcer called all cars to the track to pack the track surface for the evening racing. Steve and George were one of the first cars on the track. The track was always very muddy at the beginning of the packing process. Needless to say when the cars returned to their pit area they were covered with mud. Everyone in the pit area grabbed an implement of some kind and started cleaning; hence the name of the crew was "mud pickers"

The evening of racing and the bomber class was called to the track. Once again Steve and George were among the first to be on the track. The cars were lined up and the race started. This was not Steve's first experience of racing. We had had go-carts for several years. Steve was about thirteen when we first started racing go-carts. In fact while stationed at Charleston, South Carolina we each had a go-cart.

Steve was a much better driver than I was. I gave him the faster of the carts and we raced my times until I had a bad wreck and lost the ability to race hard. I could keep up with the other carts but I could not bring myself to get close to another cart. Finally the decision was made that we would get out of cart racing and the carts were sold.

Back to that first race, Steve was holding his own in the heat race. Getting a little bolder with each lap he drove. Four laps later while going into turn three both the front tires rolled off the rims. Too much side load and the tires had simply separated from the rims. No one had warned us, no one had told us that we needed inner tubes in all of the tires. We inflated the tires to a higher level and finished out the rest of the nights racing. Although it was much harder to drive the car and not have it slide around all over the track.

The following week all of the tires had inner tubes installed. This meant that we could set the tire air pressure much lower and allow the car to hook up better to the track.

We finished the season in the top ten of all the cars in the points race. We congratulated ourselves on having started late in the season and finishing so high in the point's race. Importunely for us this was to be the last race at the Vallejo racetrack. The owners had sold the property to a housing contractor and there were plans for many houses to be built.

The closest track to us that ran a racing division close to our style of car was the Petaluma racetrack. It was located thirty-three miles from us. We didn't know if we wanted to travel that far to race. I bought a double axle trailer, and the decision was made that we would go to Petaluma and continue having fun racing. Nothing serious we were going to have a good time and enjoy the fact of just racing.

We raced that first year, not always going to the track every Saturday night. Some place during the latter part of the season the engine decided that it did not like to run at the RPM's needed and a rod bearing started to knock. That was the end of that year. I didn't know if I wanted to build up an engine to handle the rigors of racing. The Pontatic engine did not stand up well to racing.

During the winter months while talking with Skip, he and his partner offered us a Chevy engine that was in parts. We could have it if we wanted to build up the engine. I had worked on cars all of my life while helping my father in his garage. What I had never done was build an engine from scratch. Yes I had taken engines apart. But dad always did the critical work when the engines were placed back together.

Finally I accepted the Chevy engine and made plans to convert the Pontiac car into a Chevy car. The front fender and hood were changed as well as the front bumper. The track inspector said that would be all that he required.

Skip helped me pick out a camshaft for the engine and it was ordered. Little did I know at that time how critical a part the camshaft played in the performance of an engine. The camshaft we chose produced lots of tork at low RPM's. It did not require the engine to be turning a high RPM.

We ran the street stock class and there were several restrictions on what could be changed from stock. We had to have a stock cast iron intake manifold as well as stock exhaust manifolds. The engine block had to the original cast iron and several times the engine numbers of our engine were checked to make sure that we were running a stock block.

The track also required that we run a specific two barrel five hundred cubic feet per minute carburetor. I purchased the carburetors new and took off several things that we did not need for racing. The only change that was made to the carburetors was to change the jets, dependent on what the engine required to make it run at the proper temperatures in the cylinders.

We started out the first outing with the attitude that we were going to race for the fun of it. We were not concerned about the points race to see who would be the track champion. I left the street differential in the car which had a ratio of 2.83 and it made the car a lot slower then most of the cars we raced against. We were using old street tires which did not allow the tires to hook up to the track either. Finally I had had enough of being the car that was always beat. We did not win a feature race; we didn't win a heat race.

A heat race is where all of the cars in the class are divided into three groups for what is called "heat" races. We were always in the third heat which is the slowest of all the qualifiers at the track.

I started looking around and found a 3.33 gear ratio and the car did a little better. However the only way that Steve could keep up with the fast cars was to run very high on the race track. We won one feature that year. I was determined that I would get a better differential. I started haunting every junk yard in the neighbor. Finally found one with a 3.55 ratio.

At the same time I bought twenty five wheels and needed to purchase the tire that the track now required. So we had new wheels, new tires and new inner tubes.

At the beginning of the 1984 season we are committed to a serious run at the track championship. With the best in tires and wheels, a three fifty cubic engine that produced over four hundred foot pounds of torque. An interesting point is that the engine didn't turn at a high RPM. Most of the time it was around fifty two or fifty three hundred RPM's. An almost unheard, of low rate of engine speed. All of the fast cars turned well over sixty five hundred RPM. To those that are not familiar with what speeds an engine runs at, your street car runs at between fifteen hundred to two thousand RPM.

At the beginning of the 1984 season of racing I kept meticulous notes on the building of the race car frame, the ride height of each corner of the frame. I borrowed Skip's car scales and set the weight of the car for fifty-three per cent weight to the left side. I wanted fifty three of the cars weight on the rear end of the car but could only get fifty two per cent on the rear end as compared to the front. Close to what was decreed as the best set up for racing.

At the track George played a very important part of keeping track of all the tire pressures both before the race and after the race. This may not sound like much but it requires many measurements to be made and recorded. It paid off later, as we learned how to jack weight around on the car. Without the notes we would have been guessing. To compound the information that we kept, we also had to deal with the jetting of the carburetor. Both George and I learned how to read a sparkplug so as to determine what size jets to install in the carburetor. In addition to all of this, we kept track of the spark advance of the distributor. We slowly learned what was necessary to make the car perform to the top of its ability.

George and I would walk out on the track surface to determine how sticky the surface would be for each race. As we walked back to the car we would make a decision as to what the tire pressures would be for each tire on the car. We kept track of this information as well and it went into the book I kept for the racing year.

I will just say that George and I figured out how to jack weight around so the car would handle better each time it went out on the track. If the left rear tire pressure is raised one pound, where would it affect the set-up of the car? In this case it would transfer weight to the right front tire making the tire bite better into the surface of the track. This would make the car handle better in the turns.

If the car was trying to swing the rear end out during the turns this meant that it needed more weight on the right rear tire, or reduce the left rear tire. Soon George and I had mastered the art of hooking the car up to the track surface where Steve could drive low or high in the turns; pass in-side or on the outside in the turns. Most cars did not hook that well. As the car departed the turn the gear ratio gave more bite to the track and this way Steve could accelerate as fast or fast than most of the other cars at the track. George and I had our routine down pat, he knew what I was thinking and I knew what he was thinking.

One more to add to the list that was already long. We measured the circumference of every tire and would shift from eighty six inches to ninety one inches. I must say that George was a quick study, tell him once and he had it. Our biggest challenge was reading the track and determining what and how the track would change during the evening of racing.

About two-thirds way through the racing season the track owner told me that our engine was borderline illegal. We had eleven to one compression pistons. The track owner told us that we could not race that engine again at his track. The following Monday morning I was at the local speed shop and told the owners my story of the engine not being legal. I bought a three fifty engine block and had the deck blocked. All this means is that the top of the engine block is parallel to the crankshaft. I bought a set of pistons and rods and had them balanced. We got the engine parts Wednesday evening and started to assemble everything. Thursday evening late the engine was in the car and started. I had purchased another camshaft identical to the first one in the old illegal engine. We ran the engine at high speed for thirty minutes to break the engine in.

We arrived at the race track and unloaded the race car. I had no idea how this new engine would perform. It came as a pleasant surprise that this new engine was stronger than the engine that it replaced. The car qualified faster, was faster on the track, and still had the same handling as before. During the 1984 season Steve won thirteen feature races. More than anyone else has ever done at the Petaluma race track.

We had our share and more, of engine tear downs during the season. What we learned later is the fact that a fellow that helped with the race car was telling our competition of everything questionable on our engine and the race car. No one else could have known of some items that were borderline questionable. I'll not mention his name for I don't want to give him any credence at all for all the grief that he caused.

We won a total of thirteen races yet missed the championship race by thirty five points.

I built a second race car for the 1985 season. We would be a two car team. The cars were identical in every respect. Skip had stopped driving his race car at the end of the 1984 season. It took a lot of persuading and I had to promise him that he would not have to work on the race car at all. All he had to do was show up at the race track and drive the car. He would not have to work on the car at the race track. I told him that I would take lawn chairs for him and Steve to sit in while I and the crew took care of the race car. I proved true to my agreement with him and did have lawn chairs where Skip and Steve could sit and relax and talk about racing.

For the 1985 season we set about racing as we did the year before. The difference now is that we have the experience from the previous year which was applied to both cars. Now George and I had two cars to take care of. Everything doubled from the year before. Double the sets of tires and all of the other parts we carried to the race track each Saturday night.

Out of twenty six races, twenty one races had one or the other of my race cars finishing first or second. Quite a record for someone, three years before, knew very little about racing. Steve won the championship by thirty five points, with Skip second in the points race. We had quite a racing season. My only regret is that the cars were not painted with the same paint scheme. I really wanted to have both cars identical with sequential numbers. Did not work out that way!

Steve's car was blue from the hood level and lower, orange on the roof down to the hood level. Denver Bronco's colors, I even took a Denver jacket to the paint shop and ask them to match the colors. Skips car was deep blue from the hood down with the top white. His number was 80 and Steve's had our original number 83. Incidentally that is the same number that Skip ran in the super stock class.

In closing I must say that without George we could not have accomplished all the tasks that I had set out for us. Without his help I could not have keep up with all the details of having a successful racing team. It didn't make any difference if there were one or two cars. George was my right hand, he did many tasks without being asked. He did a lot of the heavy lifting. All of the tires and wheels had to be loaded on to the tire carrier. Tool boxes put in the truck. The list goes on and on.

MY strongest gratitude goes to him and to his wife Suzi. She was the chief of the pit crew. Organized the cleaning crew, kept track of all of the qualifying times and much more. Recorded races, and how each car finished, and in what order. I must say that without George and Suzi we would not have had a winning team.

I didn't realize how much they contributed to the overall performance of the racing team. They were the most ardent fans. They could be counted on to carry more than their share of the load.

Now, some twenty years later, I realize even more now, what George and Suzi contributed. They gave their all, and to them I say thank you from the bottom of my heart.

This story is dedicated to George and Suzi and what they mean to me. What more could be said of a daughter and her husband. I love them more for what they gave and I did not appreciate at the time.

MY WIFE

RETHA M. ROBERTSON SOWDERS

Today, yesterday and tomorrow! Back one and then forward two. That is life and what we live.

With my wife's illness I do not know which way to look. On one hand I want to look forward but at the same time I want to look back as well.

We sit by the phone waiting. Waiting and watching as it appears the disease is progressing. With each day there seems to be a new ache or pain.

Wish as I may I can not take the pain away. I can not stop the hurting. I have prayed and prayed and always ask for her to be released from the disease.

Does he hear? Does he feel my pain as we wait? But always at the end of my prayer I ask his will be done.

Am I doing right praying this way? How should I reword my prayer? What can I do with each passing day?

Through out our lives we have had our ups and downs. Still I would feel lost with out her in my life.

Each day I tell her I love her. Each day I feel her pain. I need her more than words can ever express.

I want to keep her as long as possible. By my side! I need her more now than I have ever before.

Still I do not want her to suffer. I say these words and yet I do not want to turn her loose. Am I wrong? How can it be wrong to want your companion with you?

It is hard to imagine life with out her guiding hand. Her strong resolve! Her strong inner being!

As I write these words there are tears in my eyes. I can hardly see to type.

What kind of being am I to want to keep her near?

I do not want her to suffer! I do not want her in pain! If it is required I will tell her to go! Tell her to let go and make that journey.

Still it saddens me to make that statement! My heart is heavy! For I am not ready to tell her to go.

It is difficult because on one hand my heart says one thing. My mind says something different!

To be without the woman I have lived with for over fifty five years.

I am selfish! Yes, I don't mind telling you that.

I guess we all take things for granted. We get set in our familiar ways. I am no different.

I do want to keep her! I do love her and tell her with tenderness in my voice.

With each passing day she is slipping away, little by little. She gets weaker and weaker. She has more pains that come and go.

Where or what do I do but support her every whim. Be it large or small, because I could never forgive myself when the time comes.

It is coming! Yes, my heart and mind tells me so. Yet I dare not listen to them. I dare not acknowledge it in any way.

I thought it would help to write about it. Now so for, it brings it to the forefront of my mind. I have tried for so long to put it out of my mind. I thought I had.

Yet here I sit and nothing has changed. I am no closer to accepting what I know will be.

It is so very difficult to write about it. Yet I feel I must! It is so difficult!

I am no closer now than when I first began this writing. I have only caused my mind to allow the thoughts to come the surface.

Some things I do not want! I will put the thoughts away, till some other day. Push them back to where they came from.

Still I am faced with the dilemma.

How can I feel one way and not want it to change? Why can't my heart and mind agree? I do not have an answer. For there is not an answer at this time.

If I could, I would take her illness to myself. I would much rather have it be me. That has been the plan we have had, for so many years. I would be the first to go.

Now I dare not leave her. No longer can I be the first to go. She can not take care of herself any longer. She can not drive. She should never be alone. With one eye she has trouble seeing. This is what I am faced with.

Now I must stay strong for her. I must be the one to fulfill every craving or desire of her life.

No longer can I allow myself to get sick. What I have is so minor compared to what she faces.

Are there any answers to it all? I fear not, for I somehow must be able to discern what is not yet discernable.

This is what makes the whole situation so unsolvable.

I wish I could look into the future! I wish I knew the best way to direct our efforts.

Still I do not know!

She has so been looking forward to the little house with the huge garage in Ky. Making plans! Deciding what curtains to hang! What will be in each bedroom.

In her mind she knows what she would like to have. Some times I do not have that capability. There is something that stands in the way! Trying my best I can only see today. Sometimes I don't want to know what tomorrow will bring. Am I so wrong? What stands in the way?

I don't want to know!

My mind refuses to continue with this conversation. Now it has taken control, and pushed all else to the deep dark recesses of my brain.

What else can it be? I opened the door for a small amount of time. Now it is time to—what? I really do not know and my mind refuses to let me dwell on it any more.

RICHARD

What is in a name? Not much of a question is it? Still just what kind of an image does the name Rickard bring to mind?

For me it is a young man in his mid twenties. Tall, slender with wavy brown hair.

He came into the family life in the 1950s. He was attracted to my wife's next sister down from her. She was staying at our house for a while as her first marriage had ended and she needed a place to live.

Richard came calling and soon was a daily part of her life and ours.

Richard had a beautiful almost new car which was his pride and joy. For the life of me I can not remember what make and model it was. What I do remember is the 1930 Ford Coupe. Red it was and as pretty as any new car that was on the street to me.

For some reason left the Ford Coupe at our house. I drove that car everywhere. I would slide it around corners. Broad-slide it and put it into a space that I wanted the car to stop.

I guess you can say that this was the beginning of my racing career. I could just see the red coupe being directed to the winners circle. I would stand up in the seat and wave to the crowd. Boy what an imagination I had. That little red car could not beat any of the souped up coupes that were the best at the local racetracks. I know because I was there almost every weekend with my Uncle Edgar, Uncle Ethel or my cousin Wayne.

Talk about fast cars they all had fast cars for the years just after WWII.

But I digress from my subject. Richard had a love for swimming in quarry holes. My family, err, that is, my extended family because my wife's oldest brother was living with us as well. He was a good swimmer but not as good as Rickard.

I have seen Richard take a running start and dive off three ledges into a quarry hole that he had never seen before. He could move through the water like a fish. I had never seen anyone that could move as fast as he did through the water.

Soon there was talk of a wedding. And sure enough it was a wedding. Richard had popped the question to her and she accepted. Details of the wedding I forget but let me tell you there was never a happier couple than Letha and Rickard.

Years pass, children are born and soon I have three children and Richard and Letha had two boys.

Our ways part as life leads us in different directions. I joined the Navy and Richard soon became established in a local a business. Time passes and my wife and I return to Indiana to live out the remainder of our lives.

This is where Richard and I became more than just friends. He would call our house and ask "what are you kids doing?" It became almost an expected greeting, from Richard.

We had purchased a Condo and were moving into it with all of the boxes and stacks of furniture. Everything that could be disassembled for the move was disassembled. Parts taped together so they would not be lost in the move.

Richard and Dan, one of my wife's younger brothers was a god send. They helped put table legs back on. They put things together that I had forgotten about. They assembled a new stand for the TV. It came in a thousand pieces and it took all three of us to deicer the instructions and how everything was to fit.

Richard was always one that could be called upon to help with a difficult job. Be it little or small. He was always there.

Soon Richard and his wife became almost a daily part of our lives. At the drop of a hat we were ready to go out for a meal. Needed an experienced driver to take us to Indianapolis? There was Richard and Letha going with us to insure that we arrived at a Doctor's appointment on time.

Need someone to go to Kentucky with me to watch our new house and garage as construction was started. Need company to drive to Ky. again to watch concrete being poured for the floor.

Once again Richard was there with me when the walls were set in place.

Now this is a three hour drive each way to reach the site of our new summer home.

Actually my wife and I had purchased almost three acres next to our only son's property. We wanted a place where we could stay with out intruding into our son's family. That is why we have a large garage with a small house attached. Almost always it is the other way around. Big house and a small garage.

Our son needed a larger garage than what he had. We needed a small place to live. So we combined the two into one building. The living area is 575 sq. ft. and the garage is 1450 sq. ft.

Soon the walls were up and time came for the electrical wiring to be installed. Who helped, Richard and Dan were there. I had drawn the plans but it took two experienced men to actually place the electrical boxes, all of the wiring and lots more. There are overhead lights, electrical fans, smoke detectors, and all of the receptacles and switches to be installed.

Thanksgiving has come and gone for the year 2005. Christmas is upon us, all of the family gets together and going out to eat was but one of the things we enjoyed together.

We were having a family get together at our house as our youngest daughter Susan had came in from California for a short visit. What none of knew except for a scant few, was the fact that her oldest son was to join us that morning. Richard was not there yet as it was assumed that he had to work that morning.

What really happened was the fact that Rickard had gone to Indianapolis to pick up Andrew, Susan's oldest son. Arrangements could not be completed in time for her youngest son Matthew to be here as well.

Richard came in the door and greeted everyone and it seemed that he picked up a plate and started to fill it. All of a sudden there was the doorbell ringing and Andrew walked in with the biggest smile I had ever seen in the whole wide world.

Tears were shed, hugs were abundant. But who made this appearance possible? Richard, he had driven to Indianapolis to meet Andrew and bring him to our house.

Just before Christmas we all gathered at a local restraint where unbeknown to us we were to have an unexpected guest join us. I noticed that Richard was looking at the entry way door frequently. We already had our oldest daughter Joy with us as she shared Christmas season with us. Little did we expect our son Steve to join us in our festive mood.

Richard was the first to see our son Steve walk in the front entry way. Jumping up he moved quickly to guide Steve to our table. What a judicious occasion it was.

Our church was having a Christmas service Saturday night, in fact two of them one at 5:30 PM and the second to begin at 7:00 PM. My wife and I and our two children decided to attend the first service so we could get home earlier so we could visit more with each other. Richard and his wife decided to go to the later service.

Little did we know that Richard was soon to leave us! Arriving home shortly after 7:00 PM we received a telephone call that Richard was sick. Little did we know that he was gone before we were aware of his sudden heart attack!

THE WEDDING OF
JANESSA AND BRUCE

This was one of the most unusual weddings I have ever attended. First of all, there were four people doing sign language, one on each side of the church. Some of us were not aware that there were many deaf people present. There were two signers up on the pulpit with the couple. Bruce was deaf and could see one or the other signers all the time.

The wedding was to begin at 6 P.M. but it did not. I decided at 5:20P.m., to go to the wedding. These were family friends and my wife had to go to Indiana during the time of the wedding so that is why I was not sure I wanted to go. But my wife received an email shortly before telling of the wedding, so that is how this writing came about.

Figuring if I took my time I'd arrive at about 6:30P.m., in time maybe to see the last part of the wedding. Wrong!!! I left the house at 5:53P.m., and did not drive fast. I arrived at the church at 6:08P.M. That was unbelievable. Just absolutely impossible!!! I did not hit one traffic light; there was little traffic and no one in the way for a trip that should have taken me at least 20 minutes on a good day!! My plans went afoul, somewhere.

Upon entering the church sanctuary, one was amazed at the sign language taking place among the people. Probably half of the people were deaf.

There were beautiful flowers arranged gracefully on both sides of the pulpit. Great arrays of candles were centered behind the table. Lisa Cowan, sister in law of the bride, did a beautiful job of lighting the candles in her long flowing black, backless from the waist up, gown.

The table held two individual candles, which represented the couple about to wed. Between them was a single candle, which symbolized the unity of their love and lives. Later in the ceremony, the bride and groom each took a candle and lit the center candle, then blew out their candles.

There was a wonderful string quartet playing music. Those present were in a hushed state, waiting the arrival of the beautiful bride. The bride's family sat on the left and the groom's to the right in the seating area. Virginia Hall, the bride's grandmother had just gotten out of the hospital and it was questionable whether she would be up to being there. Very ill, she was there, but was taken home right after the wedding. She did not try to stay for the reception.

A photographer was present in the balcony of North Hills Baptist Church, along with George Hall, uncle of the bride, with his video camera, to take in all of the scenes as they unfolded.

The Pastor entered from the right followed by the groom. They and the people waited, turning in anticipation of catching first sight of the beautiful bride in her off-white satin gown with its beautiful long train.

Merrylynn, the bride's daughter was gorgeous in her white gown. She was her mother's Maid of Honor. She was escorted down the aisle by her uncle, Chris Cowan, who then took his place alongside the groom.

Seven Bridesmaids followed Merrylynn in their flowing long black gowns, each with a black matching scarf draped around their arms and shoulders. Several of these bridesmaids were deaf. One had a baby the day before and could not be present. These bridesmaids were escorted each with a groomsman.

Suddenly, the music stopped!! Heads turned and many stood on tiptoes to view the brides' approach. The wedding march music began!! All knew that the bride would come into view at any moment. She could now be seen moving slowly down the aisle. Slowly, the bride came into view, escorted by her father. They stopped at the foot of the altar.

He was facing the couple, then turned and was standing just in front of the pews, when he began the wedding vows. Since Bruce could not speak, he answered back through the interpreter. When it came Janessa's turn she also used sign language.

Pastor Tom Stringfellow started the service by stating he was going to preach, which he did, for about twenty-five minutes on the subject of the "3R's" (Responsibility-Respect-Result). The pastor directed his words to the bride and groom as well as to those present. Impressing upon each one present, that they were as much a part of the ceremony as the couple being joined together in the holy bonds of matrimony.

After the pastor had finished his message there was special music presented by the bride's brother, Mr. Chris Cowan and Mrs. George Hall, (the former Miss Linda Susan Sowders.) The duet was among the highlights of the entire wedding ceremony, (especially since Miss Susan happens to be my daughter.) The words were chosen so they added complete harmony to this special event. The singer's voices complimented each other and the music added complete beauty to the special song. There could not have been any better choice than these two to completely set the mood for the final words to be exchanged between the bride and the groom.

Pastor Tom then stepped forward and asked, "Who gives this woman to be a bride. Her father responded, "her Family and I do." The pastor then turned and asked the groom to come and get his bride. He walked gently toward his bride, Janessa. Together they strolled eloquently to the altar.

The bride's gown and accessories were off-white. On her head she wore an off—white tiara accented with pearls. The bridal vale trailed back, falling to her shoulders. The heart-shaped neckline accented the long gown. Large puffed Sleeves were full length with frilly one-inch lace around her slender wrists. The bodice was intricately decorated with pearl beads and glitter sequins, which also ran down into the train.

About her waist she wore a two-inch belt of white satin, with the ends falling delicately to the knees. The beautiful off-white satin gown flowed outwardly from the waist cascading to full length extending out to the train. With many folds, it made the bride stand out, as a virginal bride, at the altar.

The gown was fitted with a six-foot flowing train of matching satin, which kept her lovely young daughter busy, lifting and flowing it into a graceful train behind her mother, the bride.

The bride carried a lovely spray of white carnations, which showed the slightest hint of red along the edges of the petals. It was delicately tied with half-inch ribbon, which streamed lightly downward ten inches.

The bride's nails glistened with clear polish, which accented her lovely long fingers as she nestled the bouquet in her left hand.

Standing before the table holding the unity candle, with a smaller candle on each side which represented their past lives, the bride and groom turned to face each other. Holding hands and looking intently into each other's eyes, they lit the large middle candle, before blowing out their single candle.

There were two sign language experts standing on each side of the setting area. Facing the congregation they signed each word of the ceremony to the deaf in the pews. On the pulpit, there were two additional signers for the wedding party to watch that needed assistance in knowing what was being said.

As the pastor moved forward to ask the customary words "Do you take this woman to be your wife and helpmate, a male signer stepped just to the left of the pastor and signed to the groom. The groom signed to which the signer spoke the words for the groom "I Do".

Then the pastor turned to the bride and repeated the statement "Do you take this man to be your husband and helpmate"; the signer again translated the pastor's words. The bride signed the message and the signer spoke the words for the bride "I Do".

At this time, the couple stepped to the back of the unity table, with each taking a tabor and lighting it from their respective candles. Together they singularly touched the unity candle causing it to burst forth with a single flame, signifying their coming together as one.

The couple returned to the front of the unity table, once again facing each other. The groom took the bride's hand and rings were exchanged. The best man presented the rings to the pastor, who in turn handed them to the bride and groom. He asked each in turn to place the rings on the left ring finger.

This done, the pastor then said "by the power invested in me by the State of California and by All Mighty God, I now declare you husband and wife. You may kiss your bride."

The groom placed his arms around the bride and kissed her long and lovingly. Following this they turned toward the congregation and smiled as the pastor introduced them as Mr. and Mrs. Bruce Price.

The pastor turned to the congregation and explained that there is a custom the native 'Africans Americans' perform at the conclusion of the ceremony. It is the jumping of the broom. The bride's father and the groom's father stood and each holding an end of a broom walked to the platform. The broom was placed on the floor and the bride and groom while holding hands, jumped daintily over the broom before leaving down the aisle.

With ceremony completed, those present were encouraged to attend the reception in the Benicia Clock Tower building, in Benicia, California.

The Benicia Clock Tower dates back to the early days of California and was constructed shortly after gold was discovered there. It is a massive structure having been built with large squares of quarried sandstone. The second floor is now used often for large gatherings.

After the service was over it was announced that the wedding party would be going back inside for pictures. That took almost an hour. I was going to wait and follow my daughter Suzi and husband George to the clock tower in Benicia. But I did not!! When I arrived at the tower, there was a long line waiting to sign in. A person that could not speak or hear was in charge of the signing in book. It took about 15 minutes to get through the line.

When I got inside, there was my son Steve and wife Debbie, with their four children. There was a small line set up with salads. The kids and I went through the line and had a plate. I talked to Richard and Joyce Lindsey while waiting for the wedding group to arrive.

When the wedding couple came, they were escorted to the dance floor where two chairs were positioned and everyone was asked to circle the dance floor. It was announced that there would be a special African dance group performing. It was quite an unusual dance. Must have been a fertility dance because there were a lot of hip movements (If you get my drift). This lasted about 15 minutes.

All eyes turned toward the entryway and viewed the four dancers in their African costumes. Two men were playing drums as they led the procession toward the dance floor. First came two young black ladies followed by two husky broad shouldered young African American men.

The drummers were seated while the dancers took a stance in the middle of the dance floor, striking a pose, and holding it. A hush fell over everyone, as they waited for the dance to begin.

Fast drumbeats came forth, and the dancers moved in time with the quickened beat. The movements, with a sensuous tone lasted several minutes.

Then it was time to eat as a lot of us were getting hungry. HA the only thing wrong was that there was only one line set up and it was very slow. I looked at my watch and it was after 9 by this time. I was seated at one of the head tables. I think my daughter Susan had something to do with that. Anyway, I was way ahead of the majority of other people.

As I was waiting in line Steve came up and said that they were leaving. They did not wait for their turn for the food line. There was plenty of food, but it took such a long time before everyone was served.

I had a lot of salad and some Ravioli. What was unfortunate is that I put a salad pepper on my plate. I ate it! Guess what? I started to itch at about the same time that it went down. I went to Suzi and told her that I was going home, which I did. Took Benadryl, as soon as possible!!

Jan told me this morning that the cake was served about 11:00. The last of the people had just gotten their food before that. There was very little dancing. Matt's band played one song. A song that Chris wrote, I believe. Chris sang it.

Pat and Jan Patterson got back here about 12:30am. Suzi and George didn't get home until 2:30am. They took all of the wedding gifts and food to their house. Everyone was at Suzy's house Thursday night for supper (except me). Now that I think of it, it may have been Friday night they all came for dinner.

Mr. and Mrs. Price left on their honeymoon for a cruise trip. The whereabouts unbeknown to me.

THINKING OF YOU

Where does it all begin?
Romance has so many places
Of when you came into my life
The beautiful young woman
That captured my heart

Teasing you to get your attention
Pulling your hair
Am I getting through?
Will she see me?
As I look from afar?

Touching your beautiful hair
Trying to hold your hand
Or catch your eye
Will she like me?
My mind asks again and again

To sit next to you
To put my arm around you
Slip close and let our shoulders touch
There, I did it! A thrill runs up my back
Ah! She likes me from the smile she flashed!

TOGETHER

I am going to tackle a subject that lays heavy on my heart. It is one that shows the changes in the moral attitude of young people today.

In nineteen forty six I started liking a young lady. It was called liking because we were sweet on each other. Once again I am calling upon memories from long ago.

To put it another way this young lady was my sweetheart, my girl friend. We dated during our high school years. We were still together when we graduated from high school. During the summer of nineteen fifty we dated. We were out of school and I had a job working for the Ford Motor dealership in Bloomington. My girl friend was working at the RCA plant. Our plans were to be married in June of nineteen fifty one.

In august of nineteen fifty the draft was getting close so I joined the United States Navy. I left for boot-camp and departed Great Lakes Naval Training Center for Pensacola, Florida.

In December of nineteen fifty I came home for Christmas leave, from my duty assignment at NAAS Corry Field. I had an engagement ring in my pocket and as soon as I was with my sweetheart I gave her the ring and told her I wanted to get married as soon as possible.

We applied for a marriage license and had the necessary blood testing done. What we did not realize was the fact that the testing would take several days. I only had a seven day leave from the Navy. We were waiting on pins and needles for the blood test results to come back. That was the longest wait I have ever had and I have had some long waits in the Navy.

Finally the blood test results arrived and Doctor Mitchell called that everything was okay. We were married the next evening and departed for a very short honeymoon of one night.

I tell you all of this that I might say that not once in all of this were there ever any consideration of living together without the sanction of marriage. It never crossed my mind and I am sure that it never entered the mind of my sweetheart.

I am going to step on some toes here but I do not believe in the current state of affairs where a young man and a young woman live together without the sanction of marriage.

It is wrong and somehow someone has to speak up and tell it like it is. Young women of today some how think it is okay to live as husband and wife without the marriage sanction. Why?? What is the reason?? I really don't have an answer other than to say that it is not right.

Why would a man or woman want to live together and share the same bed with out marriage? Is it because of a breakdown of the family values of today? Maybe!!

Is it because the young women of today are afraid that they will not be able to get a man without sleeping with him first? Do the young women believe that they have to give themselves and prove that they are good in bed.

Do you know that each young man and woman have to reinvent sex for themselves? It is a strange new world and each couple has to come to know each other like no other. This is for a husband and wife to explore and know what there is to know about each other.

I think I have said enough and still I do not feel that I have properly covered the reasons and the whys of the times of today. Thousands of words could be written and maybe still not cover the subject satisfactorily. I do not profess to know and do not know of any one that can give an answer to the situation of today.

Friend,
Lover,
Mother,
Love
of my life,
My Precious
Wife

WHERE DOES IT ALL BEGIN

As I sit here thinking about it all,
I wonder just where it began!
Was it yesterday or the day before?

Perhaps, last week or the month before that.
Maybe it was last year or the year before that.
Wonder as I might I still do not know the answer.

There are moments when it seems
to go fast and then there are
moments that it all drags slowly past.

Pondering seems to do no good.
Staring into the past does not seem to help.
Where will I find what I need to know?

It is times like this that I
seem to not have an answer.
Though I strain mentally to put it all together.

Alas there still is not the least bit of
information that I can garner
to make it all come together.

Life's highs and lows are
not a strong point to make
sense of it at all.

What is it that is sought for?
What is it that would bring it
all together so that I might feel
that I know enough to realize the real meaning?

Why did this happen?
Or what caused it to be?
Where will it lead?

Answers I have none!!

But I want to know!

"Bud Sowders"

(My Grandfather)
Tombstones and Coffins
Were Gifts from Him

CHAPEL HILL-In the small cemetery adjacent to the Pentecostal Church here a number of tombstones carved to resemble tree trunks bear no mark of the master who created them. Those who have seen tree trunk shaped headstones may now know that these, at least, were the handiwork of one William Dallas (Bud) Sowders, who was born and raised here and whose body now lies at the foot of a much larger but less artistic tombstone in the sane cemetery.

Around his flower-covered grave stands a miniature picket-like fence which is painted white and carved on the stone to the left of his name is the name of Cora, his wife, who died in 1948. Bud Sowders died at the age of 55 in 1928, ending what his daughter Mrs. Mary Brown, of Bloomington described as a life in which "We felt like we knew him forever.

"Bud" was a twin. He was named William Dallas and his twin sister was named Susan Alice," Mrs. Brown said. Susan Alice married Chesley Chambers and they are the grandparents of Ross Fowler.

Although Bud's occupations were primarily farming and quarry blacksmithing, be was a "jack of all trades" and could do almost anything he wanted to do.

"I remember" Mrs. Brown recalled, one of his happier accomplishments "he took an old steering wheel from a car and set it on top of a pole in ball bearings and tied long ropes to it so we kids could have a swing. It was a Maypole, and we had never seen one and we always thought dad invented it.

When folks around the country here needed help they came to Bud. If they were in need of a casket in which to bury their dead, he nailed one together out of native pine, lined it with bleached muslin and gave it to them. The tree-trunks were for the most part also gifts to those who could not afford to buy them. "He wasn't a carver, but he carved them" Mrs. Brown said. He may not have been a carver in the strictest stone industry interruption of that job classification, but he nevertheless carved handsome tombstones.

During the First World War Bud operated a steam driven gristmill on his farm. When folks took their wheat there to be ground, and the ration stamps, which gave him federal permission to grind it, he always ground some extra, saying, "It is their wheat, why shouldn't they have enough flour. And he never charged them for grinding the extra amount.

On Saturday it was like a parade coming to our farm," Mrs. Brown recalled, "People came around from all over the county to have their wheat ground. Dad would start before daybreak and keep working until after dark. Mrs. Alva (Pearl) Rush used to come there. She'll remember those days", Mrs. Brown said Pearl walked miles from her home to Bud's mill carrying a sack of wheat on one hip and a child on the other.

Doctor George Mitchell, now deceased, used to travel by horse and buggy from his home in Smithville to tend to the sick, in Chapel Hill. Lake Monroe wasn't even a dream back then and the trip was considered short over a dirt road that cut across what is now Fairfax Beach.

Mrs. Brown as a girl, attended the valley School in that same vicinity, crossing and re-crossing the covered bridge to get there and back home. Clarence Stewart now of Ellettsville was her teacher in the old one room schoolhouse.

"The Hawkinses, Sowders, chiggers, and ragweed just about took over Chapel Hill in those days, Hanford Stewart recalled with a laugh. He

Bob' (SPEED & Sport Shop) Stewart's dad. They must have been good days, for Hanford added, 'The dirt there was so poor you had to have a pint of whiskey to raise a fuss'. George Cracraft had a chestnut orchard there then, too, and used to ship chestnuts all over the world.

Returning to Bud, he once put legs on an oil drum, cut a door into its belly, cut a hole in its top and stuck stove pipe into in and used it for a stove. "Dr Mitchell always said he invented the barrel stove," Mrs. Brown said. "It wasn't long after my dad made that stove until everybody in the country had one.

Bud made an iron man to help him cut wood with a cross-cut saw." He had a spring on that thing and every time he pulled that saw, that iron man would pull it back again," His daughter laughed.

Bud's mother was alleged to be part Indian and possessed the power to cure Thrush in infants. This was supposed to have been passed on to her son, but he never used it.

He was a man who could make anything and if he was in need of a particular tool and did not have one, he made it. Such was the case with the tools he used to carve flowers in the stone fireplace of the old Cleve Hillenburg house, a large brick home on old Ind. 37, south of Bloomington.

I was only 15 when he died," Mrs. Brown remembered, "but he was so active and did so many things for people and for us it seemed like I knew him forever.

Author Unknown

WILLIAM DALLAS
"BUD" SOWDERS

Bud Sowders is my grandfather who died before I was born.

There are many short stories I have been told concerning Bud. Bud was known far and wide, around the Chapel Hill and Sanders areas. The earliest story about Bud and Cora have them living in a small house in Sanders. Bud apparently was a blacksmith for a limestone company in the area. The house is (still there the last time I visited relatives in the Smithville-Sanders area) rather small by today's standards. It is located in the dip (valley) just north of the old church in Sanders on what would appear to be the West Side of the road.

For those that are not familiar, the Sanders area is a cluster of homes along the Smithville to Bloomington road. It is unincorporated and at the time I well remember it (1936-1950), there were about fifty to seventy-five homes in the area.

There was a general store which sold groceries and gasoline just south of the Sanders' grade school (1-8th grade). Actually the store was the first store on either side of the road if you were traveling south, after passing the Sanders schoolhouse. Land on both sides of the road belonged to different stone companies.

The store was owned by one of the Hayes brothers. I think it was Gwen. I do remember being in the store several times. It had a big wooden porch with several chairs and a rough wooden bench.

Grandfather "Bud" apparently owned the house he and his family lived in. Grandmother Cora had lace curtains on the windows. Their youngest daughter Margaret tells of flowers in the window.

I am not sure if they also had a small house across the road or if it was located on the same side as the main house. It is known that they had boarders who lived with them. Cora served them their meals. The boarders worked in the limestone quarries. Apparently they were the same quarries where Bud worked.

There are many old limestone quarries on both sides of the road, particularly on the West Side of the road just behind the Sanders school.

In the period, I have mentioned, the older quarry holes that were no longer used for quarrying were enjoyed by young and old, as swimming holes. I remember many occasions that my father would take the entire family (his brothers, sisters and all their kids as well) in a one and one-half ton flatbed truck to a quarry hole to enjoy the cool refreshing water.

I know the mothers were especially watchful of the smaller children that did not know how to swim. My sister and I were among that group. We could wade where the water was not very deep. This limited where we were allowed to get in the water. Normally the holes were cut straight down for upward to seventy-five feet depth. Only if a roadway was cut into the quarry hole, would there be places we could play in the water.

Incidentally the Olitic limestone that was quarried in this area was of the finest grade in the world.

It is not known what year this took place, but Bud came home one day and told Grandmother Cora that he had traded their property in Sanders for a wheat farm on Chapel Hill. He was enthusiastic about raising wheat and how much money they could make. When Grandmother Cora asked about the farm, some ninety acres, Bud admitted that he had not even seen the land but had made the deal to trade.

To make a very long story short, the land that Bud had traded for was not flat bottomland at all. It was located some two thirds of the way up the hill with very little flat land.

It is not known if there was a house on the farm or if Bud built the log cabin after he traded for it. My Aunt Margaret told me it had five large logs for each wall. I am not sure I was told as to how many rooms in the cabin. It did however, have a separate kitchen in which Bud purchased a sink and installed himself. He was very proud that their home was the first to have a sink for washing dishes. The fact that there was no running water in the house did not seem important, or that there was no plumbing to carry away the waste or dirty water.

Aunt Margaret does remember having closets for the dishes with glass doors. Bud was very proud to have these refinements in his home. Apparently Bud wanted to know what direction the wind was blowing. At one time he said he was tired of having to get up and determine the wind's direction. He installed a pipe up through the roof with a direction indicator inside so he could simply glance at the pointer to know the wind's direction. Aunt Margaret said that she and the other children had difficulty going to sleep sometimes because the wind indicator pole would squeak when the wind changed directions.

Bud built a gristmill on his property. It was automobile engine powered and had large stones, which ground the corn into corn meal. People of the area paid to get their corn meal ground. Many items were sometimes traded, if actual cash was not available and sometimes a portion of the ground corn meal was given as cash.

Bud also was a Justice of the Peace for the Chapel Hill area. He was reputed to be stern in meting out justice, even sometimes harsh but fair and honest. He was known as a harsh disciplinarian.

There was little cash money in anyone's pocket in those days. If someone died and the family could not afford a grave marker, Bud would make one for them. He was known for his craftsmanship as a stonemason.

Many of his markers remain today in cemeteries around the locale as a reminder of those that has passed on as well as his ability to fabricate unusual and beautiful gravestones.

All the stones being identified as Bud's are in the form of a tree trunk. Sometimes with one or two short limbs and have a variety of items setting on top of the stone. Mushrooms, nuts, birds and squirrels are there to this day as a tribute to his skills

Automobiles were new to common folks yet Bud's desire to be the first to own one in the Chapel Hill area bore fruit. Having purchased an automobile, he paraded back and forth on the Chapel Hill ridge road many times so that all in the neighborhood knew of his purchase.

Batteries then were not what they are today. Most of the time the engines were hand cranked, or the car pushed by hand or pulled by a team of horses to get the engine running.

Aunt Margaret's sister Erin, who died in February 1927 during childbirth at the age of nineteen, was most often at the wheel when their automobile was headed down hill and was assisted by her brothers and sisters to push start the car. One time, for some reason, she ran off the road and down a steep embankment. A team of horses had to be used to pull the car back up to the road. Each time Aunt Margaret related this story she laughs and tells of the good times her family enjoyed together.

During the last months Bud lived, he had to be lifted and carried from one place to another. He had what was known as Dropsy in those days. His body bloated and from what I have been told, was in great pain. Today his ailment is called congestive heart failure. Anytime Bud had to be lifted or carried, he preferred that "Eb" do it. Eb, (Everette) was my Dad.

My mother related very few stories concerning my Dad's early life. One that I remember was that my father lived a hard life under my grandfather Bud. She said that anytime Bud would get angry he would hit my father in the chest with his fist and knock Dad flat on the ground. There is not any more to this story because I do not have any other memories.

Aunt Margaret was seven years old when Bud died. She has told me several times what she remembers of that day. Bud, confined to a wheelchair, had been wheeled into the kitchen early that day for breakfast. Afterward he was moved back into another part of the house to rest. She does not remember who was present. There must have been cause for concern that his time was near. She says that my father was there and apparently was with his father when he died. Everette came out to where Margaret was sitting, told her that her dad was dead, and to go inside and pay her last respects to him! She said that Bud was lying on the kitchen table.

Someone of the family walked to the Chapel Hill general store and called Dr. George Mitchell to come to the house. When Dr. Mitchell arrived Margaret was standing outside crying and he patted her on the head and said, "Stop crying little girl", then proceeded into the house.

When Dr. Mitchell came outside some time later Margaret was still crying and he walked to her and asked, "Why are you still crying" to which she responded "My big toe hurts really bad. "Why, you have blood poisoning in that toe" and turned to one of the male members standing close by and gave instructions that they were to go to the store and get some Epson salts. Turning back to Margaret, he told her to soak her foot in very hot water with Epson Salts. Dr. Mitchell turned to those close by and stated that this young child would be dead in less than forty-eight hours if he had not taken the time to ask her what was wrong, when she was crying.

Bud died July 25, 1928.

Vernon 'Vernie" was thirty-five when Bud died. He had been married twelve years to Zelphie Arney and they had five children.

Clara "Pearl" was thirty-one at the time of Bud's death. She had been married ten years to Stanley Allen and they had two children, Ruby age eight and Morris age six, when Bud died.

Edgar was twenty-nine years old and had been married to Zonnie Kinser seven and a half years when Bud died. Their children were Robert "Wayne" age six, Leoda age four, and Loren age two, when Bud died.

Enid was twenty-six and was married for six years to Mac McClain when Bud died. She had one child, Martha age four at the time.

Erin would have been twenty when Bud died but she died during childbirth the previous year.

Everette was age seventeen and not married at the time of Bud's death. He was the oldest male still living at home. Heavy responsibility fell upon him to take care of his mother and remaining three younger siblings.

Ethel was age ten when his father Bud died.

Mary was eight years old when her father died.

Margaret was seven years old when he died.

Aunt Margaret told me the name of the undertaker that took care of her Dad's body, but since then I have forgotten. I do know he was from Heltonsville, which is six miles or so southeast of Bartlesville. I should mention that Bartlettsville is barely a wide spot in the road. Actually two roads crossed at this point.

When I was very young, perhaps five years old, I remember staying a week with my grandparents Lemuel and Lelah Sowders, (my mother's parents). Grandpa and I stopped at the store to buy something, can't remember what. At the time it seemed like a very big store. Having been in it many years later, I was surprised at how small it really was.

About 1986 or 1987 I traveled to Indiana to visit my mother, Delilah. While there, Aunt Margaret and I, and sometimes mother visited many of the cemeteries in southern Monroe and Lawrence counties. I attempted to take a photograph of every Sowder grave marker I could locate. It was during this visit that I located Jefferson Sowder's marker (described elsewhere).

Aunt Margaret and I really had a great time together that day.

Early one morning we visited the Clear Creek Cemetery where my father and mother are now buried. We parked on the eastern boundary of the cemetery. From there it is several hundred yards to the western boundary, which borders on the main Clear Creek Road.

I don't really remember how long it took to traverse this distance, but it is sloping all the way. Not steep, but nevertheless it is downhill. We had just reached the western side and I began to have angina pain. After taking nitro, which I now carry with me at all times, we sat on tombstones and talked for about twenty minutes before I felt good enough to walk back to the car. Aunt Margaret offered to go get the car but we were both afraid for her to do that since she also has heart trouble and sometimes has seizures and would faint. We laughed at each other and the predicament we had gotten ourselves into. We did make it back to the car and visited several more cemeteries before quitting that day. At the other cemeteries, we were more careful about how far we walked from the car.

TRIBUTE TO HELEN

Received an email from a dear friend who said I must write this now as it lays upon my heart. The music in an attachment reminded her of long ago times in Lemoore California. Her kind words of enjoying the music program at a little Southern Baptist Church we attended was brought back to her mind by the song. It brought more than dear memories to my heart. It opened the door for many tears.

This is a quote from the dear friend: "The music in this music makes me homesick to hear Helen Legan play and Fred Sowders sing like they did at Lemoore First Southern Baptist Church, in California. What a grand time we had there! Now I look forward to Heaven where we will get to experience that again. I do not believe I ever was in a small church with a music program like Fred and Helen developed in Lemoore. What a grand time we will have in heaven where we will all be singing God's praises along with the Angels! WHAT A GRAND AND GLORIOUS DAY THAT WILL BE!!! See you there . . . JoAnn"

To begin at the beginning it was a very small church with about 25 or so in attendance and some Sundays we had less attend. The person that was leading the music knew as little as I did about leading the music program. He was doing the best he could with what abilities he had.

I loved music but had no experience at all in leading the weekly singing service. Yet I was willing to attempt to do the best I could. I choose songs that were easy to sing. I choose songs that I knew that the congregation was familiar with.

How does one move their hands when leading music? I had no idea so I moved my hands in time with the music. Soon we were all singing together and enjoying the music portion of the program.

We did not have a regular piano player so almost every Sunday there was a different piano player. Sometimes this made it difficult to sing songs and all be together. I must laugh at this because I was so green that sometimes I felt every eye was on me to see what I would attempt to do next.

One Sunday evening there was a small group of gathered for the Sunday evening service. There was so few of us that the preacher, Brother Herald Gibson thought it best if we gathered as a small group in the back of the church. I was taken back with the few that were in attendance. We had prayer and then opened the floor for discussion. I had the impulse to present to the group that if we wanted more people to attend the church that we needed to take it to the Lord in prayer. This we did right then and there. We held hands and the words seemed to flow from each of us. Little did we know that the Lord had laid it on our hearts of what just to say. Lord send people, workers to our church.

As we were about to end our prayer the church door opened and in walked a couple new to the church. An answer already to our prayer. They joined us in our discussion and made a decision that evening to join the church.

Soon our church was growing at a rapid pace. New faces ever Sunday and almost every one joined the church. On one such Sunday a new family joined our church. I will never forget the name "Legon", the woman's name was Helen. Not only did they join the church it was soon made known that she played the piano a little. A little, my foot, she could make a piano sing. That is no joke she was good, she was outstanding. Trouble is she was good and she knew it, second trouble is that I had little musical experience and she knew it. I had played in the high school band for many years, could read music but had no experience at leading music.

Helen and I soon were at odds, she wanted to play the music the way she wanted and I wanted to lead the music the way I wanted. Finally after much thought I approached Herald and told him of my difficulties and I knew of no way to resolve the situation. Brother Herald in his slow drawl, said have you taken the problem to the Lord? Well I had to answer truthfully that I had not even considered it. So we stopped right there and had prayer. He did all the praying and I did all the listening.

Do you have any idea of how that simple prayer changed either me or Helen? I don't know who it was that changed. Maybe me, maybe Helen maybe both of us. From that Sunday morning she and I worked together. If I wanted a pause in the music, Helen followed my every gesture. Whose heart was changed? I must say that both of us changed. We were doing the music not for our own glory; we did it for the Lord.

The music program grew, the congregation grew. Soon we were having over one hundred people at each Sunday morning service. Then the number grew to one hundred fifty. The music was getting better and better. The congregation singing was getting better and better. People sang out to the Lord and he responded with more and more people.

We had over two hundred people each Sunday morning when the navy decided that I was needed elsewhere. I had orders to report to the Naval Ship Yard, Mare Island, Vallejo, California. Submarines were built there. The first of the nuclear submarines was stationed there.

I really did not want to go and leave such a wonderful church. We had such a wonderful singing program going, the congregation was really into the special times I would hold a note and soon, we had that spirit that we so desired in those moments when we asked God to add to our church. I loved Helen because she was such a help to me. With out her the music program would have been—well—a flop is the only word I can think of at this moment.

I must interject something here. Remember I said that I had no experience with leading the music. I had none zip, nada, nothing for experience. Yet we had choir practice each Wednesday evening. On one such practice I was singing along on the song and was not looking at the written music or the words. Well we came to a part that I apparently did not know the exact words so I sang saying words that were not written in the book. I must laugh because half the choir said the words I did and the other half sang what was written in the songbook. We stopped and all had a good laugh. First at the ones that said the same words that I had sang. Then we laughed at the ones that sang the proper words. Laughing we asked, those that had followed me, that they should have sang the words I did. It was a humorous moment, no one felt badly toward others. It was all taken in good spirits, but I made sure that I knew the words to sing from that time on.

Helen was the best thing that could ever have happened to our church. She was a God sent messenger. She was a wonderful and loving person. I enjoyed working with her! I thank her for all the help she gave me in learning to direct music. From the bottom of my heart, I miss her. She has gone on to be with the Lord now. Having served her time here on earth she is now in Glory Land.

SECTION V

RACING

FRED'S RACING CAREER

[My daughter Joy requested I give her a rundown of my racing career. She wanted something to help her establish where she got her start in racing, as she has been asked to speak at the Kiwanas, and is being interviewed by a racing magazine. I thought some might be interested in reading what I have written for Joy. There are some who enjoy racing talk as it is obvious Joy and I do. Maybe I have had an influence in her life after all. Fred]

Joy:

I am so glad you want to use information about my early days of racing. I will try to cover all and you can choose what you want to use.

My earliest memories of racing was sitting and listening to my Dad and his brother, my uncle Ethel. It seems dad had been to the Indy 500 to watch the race. He also went several years in a row to help direct traffic around the track. It was exciting to set there and hear all his stories.

After World War II, Dad took me to a race at the Bloomington racetrack. (I was thirteen or fourteen years old.) That was the first time I had ever seen a racecar. I fell in love with racing, with cars going fast and running close together. I knew right then, and there, that some day I would drive a racecar.

In 1955, my cousin, Wayne Souders and his father each had racecars. In those days they were called modified stocks. I went to several of these races and my desire to drive became more intense. About this time I purchased a 1938 Chevy two door sedan and started preparing it to race. The entire interior was removed except for the driver's seat. All the window glass except for the windshield was removed. A roll cage and seat belts were installed and I was ready to go racing!!

Your grandfather, Hobert Robertson, towed the racecar to the Mitchell racetrack. I was so excited!!!!!! This was to be my first opportunity to show that I knew how to drive a racecar. I was still using a regular gas tank and we forgot to put the gas cap back on when we stopped in Bedford to put gas in the car.

Doing the wheel packing on a track surface that was about two to three inches of pure mud, was great! Fast laps were even better!!! You could really hang the back end of the car out in the turns. The car was almost broadside going thru the turns.

We did time trials to determine where we would start in the heat races. I do not remember what the times were, but I was in the third heat. This is for the slowest group of cars. I did not care!!!! I was behind the wheel and anxious to get on with the race.

All the heat races were a standing start. I was in the third row inside. I was so nervous that I had trouble holding the clutch down while waiting and watching for the flagman to wave the green flag. When the green flag waved, I popped the clutch out and we were off!

Russell Roberts, a friend that was at the track, told me that I kept bumping the car in front of me all the way through the first turn. Oh well, can't expect much of a beginner that had a fast car.

I don't remember much more about that heat race except I had finished third. For my first race, that was good enough for the time being.

In the feature race, I again finished third. Total winnings for that evening, was $22.00. I got my entry fee back and paid for the gas and was ahead about three dollars. I didn't care. I had driven my first race!!

There were five racetracks within thirty miles of where we lived in Southern Indiana. I drove and raced at all of them. Mitchell, Bloomington, Paragon, Martinsville and Williams. We lived about three miles from the Bloomington track. I think I liked the Mitchell track best. I don't know why. I just felt more comfortable there.

I raced in 1955, 1956 and only a few races in 1957. At the beginning of the 1956 season, we changed the engine to a GMC 235 cu. in., six cylinders with overhead valves. The head of the engine for the car, Wayne had it milled ¼ of an inch and I installed a three quarter race cam. These engines were fast, but were limited in their top RPM.

I had to give up racing in mid-year of 1957. I just didn't have the money to put into racing, as I now was a married man with third little children. That seemed like the end of my racing career. It was, for what seemed a long time.

We moved to Memphis, Tenn. in 1962. During the summer of 1963, we were vacationing back in Indiana. Richard Lee, my brother in law, had bought a go-cart for his boys to drive. They had purchased the cart from Rex Mitchell, a classmate of your mother and mine. The engine was a racing engine but had broken down and was not repairable.

We took the cart back home with us. I was sure that I could repair the engine. At that time I thought I could fix anything. I smoothed the crankshaft somewhat and got the rod bearing where it would last a little while. The cylinder was aluminum with a thin layer of chrome. When the chrome starts breaking up there is no fix for that.

I put the engine back together and we ran it for many hours on the track that we had made in our back yard. The only thing unpleasant was whoever drove the cart would be covered with oil. With the bad cylinder, it sprayed oil badly.

Later that summer, Steve and I put a roof on the house next door to us for $100.00. That was exactly the price of a new engine for the go-cart. Just as soon as we got the engine mounted, we took the cart to the Memphis Go-Cart Track.

The engine was hooked up with direct drive. In order to get the engine started, the pusher had to pick up the rear of the cart and run a few steps before setting it down. This would be enough to turn the engine over. We ran box stock class, 6.01 cu. in. That was the max for that class. I drove in the senior division and Steve drove in the junior division. Steve got several trophies and I think I won a few.

Later at Memphis, I traded the go-cart for a motorcycle, which I then traded off for a boat. The boat was what I wanted and we had many good weekends at Sardis campground. We fished and water skied at least one weekend a month.

We then moved to Charleston, S.C. in 1966, and after a year there, I wanted to get back into go-cart racing. I purchased two go-carts with good racing engines. Again we raced box stock. I gave Steve the lighter and faster of the two carts because he was a better driver than I was. We raced part of two seasons and traveled to several different tracks. I don't remember the names of the tracks.

I had built a trailer to haul the two carts. It started out as a boat trailer. It looked really neat being towed behind our truck and camper.

We later moved to Lemoore, California in 1972. The carts were shipped along with our furniture in piano crates. Strange, we had three pianos!! There was another large box that had wheels and axle for the trailer. We put the trailer back together and used it the entire time we raced.

There were two tracks that we raced around Fresno. I don't remember the name of one of them however. One was called the River Go-Cart Club. We raced there several times. However the drivers were rough and didn't mind wrecking someone.

This is the track where I had a bad wreck. I don't remember much about it but was told that the cart flipped end over end many times. I was not seriously hurt, only had some bumps and scrapes. The other driver didn't fair as well as he had a broken leg. After that I drove a couple of times. For some reason I could not run close to another cart. I could follow and run as fast as anyone but stopped racing go-carts at that time.

In 1979, we were now living in Vallejo, California. There was a racetrack three blocks from our house where they ran street stocks, super stocks, and super modifier's. Steve still had the racing urge and we went to the races often. He owned a 1968 Pontiac and wanted to try his hand at racing in the bomber class. The engine was stock but we had a great year.

We didn't start racing until June of that year and still finished 9th in points. As it turned out, that was the last year that races were conducted at the Vallejo Race Track. The closest track now was at Petaluma, which was 33 miles away. Our 1980 season was not much. We didn't go every weekend and then when we decided we wanted to do more than just fun race, the engine broke and that was the end of that year

I do not think we raced much for a year. Keeping the same car, we put a 350 cu. in. Chevy engine in the car and changed the front fenders and hood to look like a Chevy. In 1983, Steve won his first feature race. I had the differential geared too high and he could only go fast when he ran up high on the track.

In late 1983, I found a used differential with gear ratios that were more to what we needed. It had 3.23 gears and the engine pulled well with them. Still not what we needed, but this was a lot better. Almost all of our spare parts came from junkyards. I knew the underside of many wrecked cars back then.

In April of 1984, I finally found a differential with 3.55 gears. I had built up a completely new engine. I had it bored out to .030 over standard. Had the engine balanced and got a really good torque cam. This engine made lots of torque starting at two thousand RPM right up to 6300 RPM. We were using small chambered heads and had a compression ratio of 12.65 to 1. The engine developed about 400 foot pounds of torque and had over 360 Horse Power

In 1984 Steve won 13 feature events and missed the championship by 35 points.

In 1985 Steve won 8 feature races and won the Track championship.

In 1986 we missed winning the track championship by 4 points

In 1985 I owned two racecars, Skip Brown, a young neighbor super stock driver, drove the second car. It was a tight race all season between my two cars, because they were the best of the racing field. Skip missed the championship by 35 points when Steve won the title . . .

During the 1987 season we again had two cars racing. There were several drivers that year for the second car. We let pit crew members drive. Suzi drove in several regular races. There was also the mechanics race, which George drove and did a great job. Then we had the powder puff races in which you got to race against your sister. She did beat and bang you a little

In 1988 we bought our present home, which was a fixer upper and was busy most of the year. I was cutting up a new body for the racecar when I started have angina. This was the beginning of another bypass surgery. Steve was also experiencing lots of back pain.

Most of our last years of racing are on video. I get to go racing in my family room quite often.

In 1989 a young man purchased both cars and all of the spare parts. It was hard to believe that our racing career was over. I almost cried seeing the cars and parts leaving the driveway. AND NOW I HAVE A DAUGHTER THAT HAS THE RACECAR FEVER. I am sorry that I do not live closer to her and her husband so I could be one of their best supporters.

ABOUT THE AUTHOR

Fred's motto for life is: "don't put off to tomorrow if you can do it today". He and his family went more, did more than just about anyone you may know. While stationed at the Naval Air Station at Memphis, Tennessee Fred bought a used go-kart from his brother-in-law, Richard Lee. The family was living in a nice three-bedroom brick home. The lot was large enough that he and his children built a small track for the kart and soon his son Steven was traveling at a high rate of speed. Fred would put a large cardboard box on the track. The objective was to come as close to box as possible, yet not hit it.

After a short period of time a box stock legal engine was purchased. Soon he and Steve were racing at the Memphis Go-Kart club. Steve won several races and Fred, well he got a trophy or two. Later the kart was traded for a motorcycle. Then the motorcycle was traded for a boat.

The family was transferred to Charleston, South Carolina, where the boat was put to good use. First there was water-skiing, then fishing. Then two go-karts were purchased and both father and son raced at several tracks.

The boat was sold when Fred received orders to the Lemoore Naval Station located in the middle part of California. While there he and Steve continued racing the karts. Finally Steve was old enough to get his drivers license. Life changed to include girls, cars were a major concern, and several were purchased. Steve drove many makes of cars.

Fred finally was able to get his private pilots license, something that he always wanted but could not afford! Quickly he soon had a commercial license and followed that with an Instructors license as well.

Fred had a heart attack in the early part of nineteen seventy-eight. Never to fly commercially again!

He returned to his training while in the Navy and was soon working for a management company who furnished all the personnel for Japan Airlines flight training center. He retired in 1999.